SEEK THE LOVER WITHIN

Lessons from 50 Spiritual Leaders

Volume 1

by
Tuula Fai

50 Interviews: Seek the Lover Within: Lessons from 50 Spiritual Leaders (Volume 1)
Copyright © 2010 by Tuula Fai
http://spiritual.50interviews.com

ISBN: 978-1-935689-05-8
Library of Congress Control Number 2010924041

Published by
Wise Media Group
444 17th Street, Suite 507
Denver, CO 80202
www.wisemediagroup.com

WISE
MEDIA GROUP

Based on original *50 Interviews* concept by Brian Schwartz.

First edition. Printed in the United States of America.

Dedications

To my grandmother, Sophia Klinker, who gave me unconditional love and passion for life.

To my mother, Elaine Hoiska, who taught me how to write and pursue my dreams.

FOREWORD

We live in a time when the globalization of our awareness is expanding by leaps and bounds. We're becoming ever more conscious of the staggering varieties of people on Earth and their different standards of living. We're flooded with knowledge of myriad religious beliefs and cultural practices, and with the ignorant fears and dangerous superstitions that threaten our collective survival. It's easy to feel overwhelmed, or even hopeless, when confronted with the diversity, fragmentation, and conflict that seem apparent on the surface of things. How will we ever understand each other and learn to live together without destruction following constantly in our wake?

To find an answer, we must first consider the possibility that there is an answer, and that reframing the problem is necessary for discovering it. We might consider the idea that diversity has a positive purpose, that our exploding global consciousness is occurring with perfect timing so something better can happen. Instead of looking at our differences as fodder for defensive action, we might see them as helpful. To find an answer we must ask new questions. Questions like: What do we all have in common, in spite of our differences? How can we see ourselves each as an integral part of a higher, more unified awareness? How can we see each other as aspects—unmaterialized, potential aspects—of our own greater self? And how can we then understand and trust the flow of intent, knowledge, and action through all of us, by all of us, and for all of us?

Tuula Fai has begun this reframing and questioning process here in *Seek the Lover Within: Lessons from 50 Spiritual Leaders*, by going directly to the wisest people she could find and talking to them about what they see as important today, about what they learned for themselves and how they learned these core lessons, which may indeed be universal among all peoples. What may have begun as an innocent desire to represent the views and wisdom of spiritual teachers became an experience that changed Tuula, cutting through her identification with her very bright mind and putting her squarely in the center of her heart's much broader understanding of unity and ability to engage with life. I know this because I've watched how the process of writing this book has opened her to a new sense of self, and in a very short time.

I don't think anyone can be exposed to wisdom and compassion so repeatedly and not have the resonance of those clear states bring them, too, into that higher frequency. It's like Meister Eckhart said, "When the higher flows into the lower it transforms the nature of the lower into that of the higher." That is what Tuula's adventure in interviewing did to her, and it's what a thoughtful, mindful reading of the interviews presented here can do for you as well.

As you read and "feel into" each interviewee's unique path you will no doubt see your own path to wisdom and compassion by contrast. You will see how your path is as valid and interesting as everyone else's, and you will come to value your own expansions and contractions, as well as the bends and turns your road has taken. You will find common territory with the interviewees, too, and you will be able to see past the supposedly "negative" things that have happened to you to the hidden higher purpose in your experiences and how your soul has always been helping you learn to clear your mind's blind spots.

The people Tuula chose to interview in this book are of various ages and come from different backgrounds and from faiths the world over. They use a wide variety of physical, mental, and spiritual practices to maintain their clear awareness and to empower their continuing personal evolution. These "spiritual teachers" live their message by putting their love and insight into action, both for their own pleasure and for the benefit of others and the planet.

Tuula shows us that a spiritual leader doesn't have to be famous. He or she can be anyone—a poet, minister, artist, adventurer, business leader, doctor, or school teacher—anyone who lives a life of love, service, and dedication to inner growth with tangible results. I call these people "practical visionaries," those whose feet are firmly planted on the ground, who love the earth and all the magnificent creations here, and whose heads are in heaven, communing with the collective consciousness of all souls, all beings, all planets, all solar systems. These people are often translators or bridges between the visible and invisible realms, helping those of us who have temporarily forgotten who we really are to reconnect with deeper truth.

Spiritual leaders help reveal a way to live based on how consciousness in the spiritual realm actually functions. At some point along the way, they choose to use themselves as a laboratory for experimenting with the effects of raising the frequency of consciousness—to make their own lives symbolic representations of truth that continually expand as revelations are revealed to them. By bumbling around and making many mistakes, they learn to increasingly live in accord with universal laws—principles of energy and awareness—because doing so encourages the experience of harmony and flow, which produces the feeling of joy, which feeds the genius of the creative mind, which nurtures generosity and appreciation, which helps build a physical reality that shimmers with vitality.

Spiritual leaders have learned that mistakes are just steps along the path and contain as much valuable insight as successes. They have discovered that to be in divine love with oneself and others, it is most natural to embrace every part of life, to be fully present in each moment, enjoying our bodies and demonstrating love in action. This way of being isn't about being perfect or "right"; it's about seeing each moment as perfect and our presence and actions in any given moment as "just right."

As I started writing this, I began to say that we often fall into the thought that our planet may not survive, that we ourselves may not survive, due to our negativity toward what and who we define as separate and different from us. Certainly, this is one view, and perhaps it serves as a loud alarm bell to wake us up. But the real issue at hand is not so much about survival as it is about the ongoing process of evolution and enlightenment. Spiritual leaders know that the soul is eternal, that death is an illusion. I once attended a talk by Krishnamurti, not long before he died, as he sat in an apple orchard in Ojai, California, draped in a blanket. He said, "The only death is ego." And I knew that was right, for when we're caught in fear, which creates ego, we cannot feel the true limitless life of our soul, and that truly is a death of awareness.

So the big issue now is: How will we use this time of excruciating energetic pressure? Will we break through to higher frequencies of awareness and compassion and take reality with us or will we squeeze the flow down into a tight thread of hate and irritation that must explosively break through old calcified realities like mounting water behind a cracked dam?

Seek the Lover Within contains a wealth of wisdom that can help you shift out of the old fear-based, difficult, survival oriented reality into a fluid, love-based way of living that will take you further into your own enlightenment process. Before you know it, you too may find yourself being a spiritual teacher and leader. You may find that others soon look to you for a better model of living. This is what it's all about—sharing the stories of our life experience with each other and learning. By having these conversations, and by listening and considering new ways of being, we find the common human elements and our amazing complementarity. Eventually, the big experience of Unity is revealed. And once that registers fully in you, you and the earth can move into enlightenment together.

-Penney Peirce, Intuitive and author of several books including
FREQUENCY: The Power of Personal Vibration

CONTENTS

*"What's bad is good.
It helps you find your center."*
- Stanford Addison

INTRODUCTION

Book ideas are strange and interesting things. Sometimes they sit with us for a while before coming into being. I first got the idea to write this book in 1992 when I sustained a debilitating injury from my obsessive long-distance running.

I was running in an attempt to escape the fear and emptiness I felt inside. Author Kathleen Norris calls this feeling acedia. It eventually overtook me in the form of a crippling illness that left me in great pain. After many doctor visits, I finally ended up at an HMO's pain management unit where the physician told me, "There are gray areas in medicine. Unfortunately, you are one of those gray areas." She then talked to me about using pain medications and a walker or wheelchair.

Luckily, a little voice inside said, *Her heart is in the right place but that won't be your path. Keep searching.*

I kept searching but still couldn't find anyone who knew what was wrong with me. One night I gave in and took seven of the pain pills the physician had prescribed. I later found out this was too many and I could have died! Maybe I secretly wanted to die because the pain and uncertainty of my condition were almost unbearable. Before I slipped into a drug induced sleep, I said, "God, please help me! I can stand the pain if you show me what is wrong and how to fix it."

The next morning I woke up and had a feeling that I should go to the bookstore. I hobbled my way over there and found a book called, *Pain, Pain Go Away* by William J. Faber. In it, I learned about a treatment called prolotherapy for healing damaged ligaments. When I read about the causes and symptoms of ligament damage, I realized they were exactly what I was experiencing.

The book listed osteopathic physicians who offered this therapy around the U.S. None were in Boston where I lived. So I opened the yellow pages and called every osteopath until I reached Dr. Charles Radbill, who had been doing prolotherapy for fourteen years. Dr. Radbill, and a chiropractor named Dr. James Kerner, confirmed that my ligaments were chronically overstretched and torn. Both were able to help me—Dr. Radbill with prolotherapy and Dr. Kerner with applied kinesiology and nutritional supplements. Soon after, I learned that Norman Cousins, author of *Anatomy of an Illness*, had a similar connective tissue breakdown and cured himself with laughter and vitamin C.

These therapies, along with massage, acupuncture, and herbs, got me about sixty percent better—enough to walk, return to college, and live with manageable pain. Then on the subway one day, I met Marcia. She noticed I was wearing wrist guards and asked what was wrong. I told her about my damaged ligaments and she suggested I see a psychotherapist named Jamy Faust (interviewed in book two of this series) who did Barbara Ann Brennan energy healing

In a self-righteous tone, I replied, "That psychology and energy stuff is for some people. Not for me."

I laugh at this response now because it was to become my life's work. But I wasn't ready at that time.

A year later, I called Jamy for an appointment. When she laid hands on me, I felt warmth in my body for the first time. I had been so frozen and so reticent to even be in my own skin. With her touch, I was able to return to my body and feel its nourishing resources. During our sessions, it became clear that spiritual and emotional issues had created my physical symptoms. As I dealt with these, everything in my life started to improve, including my health. I began to meditate, practice tai chi, and learn CranioSacral Therapy and Reiki. I still practice CranioSacral Therapy. It has given my clients wonderfully beneficial effects.

One morning I started shaking uncontrollably during meditation. I opened my eyes and saw a shimmering white light that said, "Don't worry my child, you will heal." I knew immediately that it was Jesus.

Six months earlier I had been at a church service where, out of the blue, a Harvard divinity student said to me, "Jesus will heal you." She said it with such compassion that I believed her.

And now here he was. I was overcome with unconditional love and a feeling that I was one with everything. The statement that Jesus made was no idle promise. Shortly after his visit, I completely healed.

This book series was born out of my suffering and searching. I wrote it to help others avoid the pain I went through by giving them resources to find their own answers. These resources consist of interviews with fifty of today's top spiritual leaders. The first twenty-five interviews are in book one; the second twenty-five are in book two. The leaders have experienced a wide variety of challenges in their lives and have used them to cultivate more awareness, love, and compassion. That is what is available to us. Pain is a gift that shows us where we need to put our attention in order to grow.

People have asked why I chose these particular spiritual leaders. I selected individuals who are the authority in their own lives, who listen to their inner guidance—the God within—and act from this place. This enables them to consciously choose their life experience. What they choose is love. Their thoughts and actions reflect this and in so doing, "bear good fruit." (Matthew 7:18) That's the test. We can claim we are acting from God, from love, but if we create more fear and separation, then we're not. That's how we know terrorists and other extremists are not living God's will. If they were, they wouldn't promote violence. As Sarabjeet Kaur (interviewed in this book) of the Sikh faith says, "God would never ask us to hurt others in his name."

Since these leaders are from diverse faiths, they have different concepts of God. However, the concepts share a common root of love and service. As Paul teaches in the Bible, ". . . You were called to freedom . . . use your freedom . . . through love [to] serve one another." (Galatians 5:13-5:14) Jesus shows us how essential love is when he says, "Love the Lord your God with all your heart, with all your soul, and with all your mind." This is the first and greatest commandment. The second is like it: "Love your neighbor as yourself." All the law and the prophets depend on these two . . ." (Matthew 22:38-22:40) In this passage, Jesus is saying that when we come from love, we come from God.

But it's not enough to just believe in this ideal. Jesus challenges us to practice it by advising, "Love your enemies, do good to those who hate you . . . To the person who strikes you on the cheek, offer the other as well . . . Treat others in the same way that you would want them to treat you." (Luke 6:27-6:31) This Golden Rule is present in almost every religion. That's because it is what you must master to be the spiritual leader of your life. As Gary Zukav, bestselling author of *The Seat of the Soul* says, "If you wish the world to become loving and compassionate, become loving and compassionate yourself. If you wish to diminish fear in the world, diminish your own. These are the gifts that you can give."†

In each moment of your life, you have the choice to act from love or fear. When you act from love, you are a spiritual leader. Your personality is aligned with your soul. You embody what Zukav calls the intentions of your soul: harmony, cooperation, sharing, and reverence for Life. You can confirm this not only by the fruits you bear, but also by how you feel in your body. When you come from love, you feel joyous, open, flowing, and con-

---

†Reprinted with the permission of Simon & Schuster, Inc., from THE SEAT OF THE SOUL by Gary Zukav. Copyright © 1989 by Gary Zukav. All rights reserved.

nected. When you come from fear, you feel stress, pain, restriction, and separation. This discernment is what Zukav, and his partner Linda Francis, teach in their Authentic Power Program. I enrolled in this program because I realized how critical authentic power is to becoming the spiritual leader of my own life. I also began studying Buddhism because Buddhists really emphasize the practice of loving your enemies. For me, this practice is one of the best ways to cultivate spiritual leadership and authentic power because it challenges me to be loving and responsible no matter how tempted I am to react in fear.

The modern story that best exemplifies this practice is one told in the book *Emotional Awareness* by the Dalai Lama and Paul Ekman. In it, His Holiness talks about a Tibetan monk who was imprisoned in China and had confided in him that he felt a deep sense of fear and danger. The Dalai Lama asked, "What kind of danger?" The monk replied, "The danger of losing my compassion . . . for the Chinese prison guards." Ekman asked if this level of compassion was something we should all be aiming for. The Dalai Lama said, "The goal is to develop an outlook in which you fully realize the interdependent nature of your well-being with that of others, and of your interests with others' interests." In other words, yes. We can all strive for this level of understanding and compassion.

On a personal level, the monk's example amazed me. Like Jesus on the cross, he was able to forgive his persecutors and have compassion for them. Some of my Christian colleagues say that Jesus was able to do this because he is God, to which I reply, "Yes, and so are we." As Jesus said, "Greater things than this shall ye do." (John 14:13) So we have the choice to respond in love, no matter how trying the circumstance. Does it mean that we always will? No, but that's the standard we should strive for—to make our enemies our lovers—and to have compassion for ourselves when we fall short.

So how exactly do we make enemies lovers? The first step is

developing awareness that there is no enemy outside us. Our enemy is our own lack of consciousness and love. I first realized this during my injury when I saw that freeing myself from habitual fears led to restored health.

I learned this in a deeper way many years later when my friend Jack introduced me to the book *Zero Limits* by Dr. Ihaleakala Hew Len and Joe Vitale. In it, the authors talk about a Hawaiian spiritual practice called Ho'oponopono. The book says that our job is to continually clean out patterns and fears that prevent us from living God's inspiration. Whenever we encounter these patterns or fears, we are to say, "I love you. I'm sorry. Please forgive me. Thank you." We are saying this to ourselves, to the divinity inside that knows everything we experience is our responsibility.

This is a radical concept of love. It means I am responsible for clearing out anything that causes pain, conflict, and separation. It also means there is no one to blame. I am responsible for it all—my injury, my CranioSacral Therapy clients' pain, the Tibetan monk's imprisonment in China, Jesus' crucifixion, and so on. And by reading these words, you now become responsible too. And you may also better understand the Golden Rule. It is not simply an admonition to do unto others what you would have done to yourself, but a bold statement that what you do to others, you do to yourself. This is because there is no out there and in here. We are all one. As Tim Freke and Greg Mooers (interviewed in this book) say, "We are one consciousness living in six billion people." So with this knowledge, why would we ever want to hurt each other?

Oneness is discussed by many of the spiritual leaders interviewed in this book series: Muslims (Laleh Bakhtiar), Jews (Rabbi Anat Moskowitz), Christians (Diana Peters), pagans (Christina Rose), Sikhs (Sarabjeet Kaur), shamans (Jorge Luis Delgado and Melanie Mulhall), kahunas (Laurie Grant), New Thought spiritualists (Linda Potter), and disciples of Indian masters (Janet Attwood and Skip Lackey). There are even those who boldly call themselves non-duality oneness practitioners (such as filmmakers Chad Cameron and Isaac Allen).

With all these spiritual leaders talking about oneness, it seems our world is on the verge of coming together in God's love. As we live out this knowing, whole new avenues become possible for resolving the issues we face. Our first step is learning to love the enemy within. Dr. Deepak Chopra told me this one evening after his talk on quantum physics. I had asked him what he thought of the book title, *My Enemy is My Lover*, when he replied, "A better title would be *My Enemy is Myself*." He then reflected on Michael Jackson's tragic death saying that even Michael, a global pop star, had a little voice inside that said he wasn't good enough.

It seemed that Dr. Chopra was pointing out a rift that existed in Michael Jackson that exists in many of us. Jackson wrote the song, "Man In The Mirror," in which he talks about changing himself to change the world. Like Jackson, we know this type of self-change is essential to being spiritual leaders in our lives. So what gets in our way? Fear. Many of the spiritual leaders in this book series agree. They see fear as being the greatest challenge facing society. It is such a challenge that Medicine Woman Marilyn Youngbird (interviewed in book two of this series) says it causes people to give away their power. Instead of trusting their own knowing, they follow somebody else's and in so doing, abdicate responsibility for their lives.

I didn't write this book so you would follow its spiritual leaders and do what they say. I wrote it so their examples can inspire you to live your own truth. As the Bible says, "The kingdom of God lies within." (Luke 17:21) Your authentic power lies within. You have all the divine wisdom you need to choose love over fear. Use this wisdom to befriend your enemies, even those voices inside your head that keep you from loving yourself and others the way God does.

As Skip Lackey (interviewed in book two) of Brandon Bays' The Journey says, "It's time to release these silent saboteurs." Once released, you can embrace who you truly are: an image and reflection of the divine. By embracing the God within, you can be the spiritual leader of your life. You can share your gifts in love and service and realize your boundless potential. As Mother Teresa said, ". . . do something beautiful for God." Only you know what that is. Only you can do it. Now, go for it!

To Life,
Tuula Fai, Denver, Colorado
Valentine's Day 2010

"Our enemies provide us with a precious opportunity to practice patience and love. We should have gratitude toward them."

- Tenzin Gyatso, The 14th Dalai Lama

"Our greatest challenge lies within our own minds and hearts."
Professor Mohammed Abu-Nimer, American University School of International Service

Mohammed Abu-Nimer is a professor in the International Peace and Conflict Resolution program at American University's School of International Service. He is also the director of the Peacebuilding and Development Institute. An expert in peace, dialogue, and conflict resolution, Dr. Abu-Nimer has conducted research among Palestinians and Jews in Israel and other areas in conflict. His work has focused on the Israeli-Palestinian conflict and on the application of conflict resolution models in Muslim communities. Dr. Abu-Nimer has also conducted inter-religious conflict resolution training and interfaith dialogue. In the last decade, Dr. Abu-Nimer has completed numerous evaluations and reports on peace building and development programs. As a scholar and practitioner, he has been intervening and conducting conflict resolution workshops in areas throughout the world, including Palestine, Israel, Bosnia, Nepal, Sierra Leone, Pakistan, Egypt, Northern Ireland, the Philippines (Mindanao), Sri Lanka, and the United States. He is the author of numerous books, including *Unity in Diversity: Interfaith Dialogue in the Middle East, Interfaith Dialogue: A Guide For Muslims, Contemporary Islam: Dynamic, Not Static, A Shared Future: Local Capacities for Peace in Community Development, Muslim-Christian Conversations For Peace.* He also has published articles in the *Journal of Peace Research*, the *Journal of Peace and Changes*, and the *American Journal of Economics and Sociology*. Dr. Abu-Nimer is the cofounder and coeditor of the *Journal of Peacebuilding and Development*. He has a PhD from George Mason University and an MA and BA from Hebrew University. He is fluent in Arabic, Hebrew, and English.

Q. What experiences put you on your spiritual path?

A. I am a Palestinian who grew up in Israel. As an ethnic and religious minority, I had to reach out to the majority to survive. So from an early age, I learned how to interact with people who were different from me. I was also politically active, working to promote equal rights for Palestinians. This activism involved preserving the cultural identities of both Muslims and Christians living in the Jewish state. In addition, my grandfather and father contributed to community mediation, *sulha* as it is called in Arabic. As a result, going into conflict resolution and peace building was a natural evolution for me. My commitment to this work grew during the ten years I lived in East Jerusalem, the part of Jerusalem that is referred to as occupied territories by the United Nations Security Council.

Q. How did these experiences change you?

A. In 1989, I came to the United States after twelve years of helping to promote peace between Arabs and Jews. American society really opened my eyes to diversity. People from different ethnicities, races, and religions were living together here peacefully. However, this peace had come through the struggles of minorities such as Native Americans and African Americans, especially during the Civil Rights Movement. My doctoral thesis was influenced by the work of these civil rights leaders. Seeing that their faith was an integral part of their struggle helped me appreciate the spiritual dimension of social change. After earning my PhD, I got a teaching position at Guilford College, a Quaker school in North Carolina. The faculty and community there really supported my work, so I felt a renewed sense of dedication to helping resolve conflict and build peace.

Q. What has been the most challenging part of your path?

A. First, overcoming the biases of exclusion and egoism that have been planted in me since I was a child. Second, creating economic security for my family. As a first generation immigrant, I struggled to economically survive for the first ten years of my life here in the U.S. Third, containing my anger and sadness when I can't seem to help people who are trapped in their pain and fear. For example, I recently chaired a panel on conflict resolution in which Sri Lankans were discussing their country's coming out of its thirty-year civil war. Not one of these people, who now all live in the U.S., saw anything wrong with how the recent war was conducted, even though since the early 1980s, over 80,000 people have died and another 300,000 have recently been displaced. It pained me to sit there for over an hour and not hear a single criticism about their leaders' handling of the conflict against the Tamil civilians and the Tamil Tigers. Similarly, I often work with Israeli and Palestinian participants and observe how difficult it is for such groups to reach a place of mutual acknowledgement and recognition.

Q. What is your earliest memory? Why do you remember it?
A. My earliest childhood memory is being taught basic math in our one bedroom home by my father who had just returned from a twelve hour day of construction work. I remember it because it reminds me of the importance of education for survival, especially for minorities like the Palestinians.

Q. Who are your mentors? What have you learned from them?
A. Vernie Davis, an anthropologist and Quaker who is the Professor and Director of Peace and Conflict Studies at Guilford College. He is a friend and colleague who has supported my work since the 1990s, when I taught at the college. Since that time, I have been involved in many different conflict resolution and peace building initiatives, some secular and others faith-based. Working with him inspired me to learn more about how to listen and be compassionate to others, especially those who I disagreed with. Said Abudul Aziz, a professor at American University, is another colleague and mentor who has been teaching over fifty years. Working with him has inspired me to pursue a unique spiritual path, which is

MOHAMMED ABU-NIMER

3

often rejected by academic establishments. Finally, my partner Ilham Nasser, who has supported my work and allowed space in our joint life for growth and independence. Her compassionate way of listening to people she cares about is something I have learned from her.

Q. What is the greatest challenge facing society?

A. Our greatest challenge lies within our own minds and hearts. We must expand our understanding in order to identify with those who are different from us and live with them peaceably. This requires managing conflict constructively and distributing resources fairly. When we fail to do so, we end up hoarding wealth, exploiting the environment, and committing crimes against each other—all in the name of self-protection and self-interest. We see this in places like Israel and Palestine. I have worked in conflict areas all over the world. In these places, I see us struggling to create space in our minds and hearts to respect each other and the environment so we can come to understand that self and collective interest are one in the same. This is my life's work. It is both highly challenging and rewarding. Each small success gives me hope that we can improve our world.

Q. What advice would you give someone just starting his or her spiritual path?

A. I encourage people to operate from their own voices, whether they are religious or secular, in order to promote peace and pluralism. For example, a Christian can foster peace after the horrendous attack on soldiers at Fort Hood, Texas by reminding people that Jesus taught us to love our neighbors as well as our perceived enemies. Also, Muslim organizations quickly condemned this attack saying it went against their faith. These are positive ways of bringing one's faith in to resolve conflict and build peace. Unfortunately, some religious people are less tolerant of those who hold different beliefs. This lack of tolerance causes them to use their faith to impose their views on others, or to justify provoking or excluding them. We see this among some groups who blamed the Fort Hood tragedy on all Muslims rather than on the disturbed individual who committed the crime. Using one's religion to impose beliefs or to provoke or exclude others runs counter to the true spiritual meaning of faith, regardless of whether that faith is Christianity, Judaism, Buddhism, Islam, and so forth.

Q. What are your practices for connecting to your higher purpose?

A. My belief system is based on the Islamic Sufi tradition. However, I have worked with Christians, Jews, and Buddhists all over the world and appreciate the contributions of their faiths as well. Unfortunately, the over-ritualization and literal interpretation of religious scripture has, to some extent, done great damage to the spiritual message of each faith. I've seen this among Buddhists in Sri Lanka during the civil war, Catholics in Rwanda during the genocide, and Jews, Muslims, and Christians in the Middle East during the Israeli-Palestinian conflict. In these disputed regions, we see people who claim to have mastered their faith but their behavior and actions indicate otherwise.

Q. How do you use these practices when you get out of balance?

A. I wish I could remain calm and centered throughout the day, but sometimes my frustration, helplessness, and hopelessness get to me. Perhaps I wouldn't appreciate being peaceful if I didn't have these moments. When I feel despair, I try to refocus my mind on the beauty and gifts that are all around me. My family, friends, and colleagues also remind me of these gifts and this really helps. These relationships, and the small successes we have built over the years, sustain me when I am in a war zone surrounded

> "Our greatest tool for human connection is our smile."

MOHAMMED ABU-NIMER

5

by hatred, exclusion, perpetrators, and victims. In addition, I do believe that within each person is a peaceful space for human connectedness, if we only learn how to unlock the doors of this inner space.

Q. How do you balance planning with remaining open to opportunity?

A. I make plans but they are always subject to change. That's because I try to keep my heart open to opportunities as they arise. It's part of my living in creativity and possibility. However, my approach can present challenges for those around me. But it's my way.

Q. If you received $100,000, how would you spend it?

A. I would give it to some people working for peace in a conflicted region. I'd probably select five or six people who are really making a difference. Then, I'd say, "Here's some money. Do something with it to support your efforts." This is the first possibility that comes to mind.

> "Using one's religion to impose beliefs or to provoke or exclude others runs counter to the true spiritual meaning of faith."

Q. If you had thirty seconds with someone in an elevator, what three things would you tell him or her to do to be joyful, peaceful, and whole?

A. First, I would smile at them. Our greatest tool for human connection is our smile. Second, I would tell them to nurture their relationships with people close to them. Third, I would encourage them to get involved in something to help others in the world.

Q. What books or resources have helped you the most? Why?

A. I read a lot of modern (Hanna Mina, the Syrian novelist) and classic Arabic literature. I particularly like the thirteenth century Persian poet Jalal ad-Dīn Muhammad Rumi. I also find modern writings by people working for peace to be very inspiring. People like Jawdat Said, an Islamic scholar from Syria who writes about nonviolence and Elise Boulding, a Quaker sociologist who is one of the founders of the peace studies movement in America. I also find the teachings of Dr. Martin Luther King, Jr. and Mahatma Gandhi to be very uplifting to the human spirit.

Q. What would you like to be written on your tombstone?
A. "Mohammed Abu-Nimer and his work have helped us to deal with pain and enjoy life." That I was able to touch their lives in a way that eased their suffering and helped them strive for peace. My legacy will be to leave behind people and relationships that work together to end our wars and create a better world.

MOHAMMED ABU-NIMER

"I have found the paradox, that if you love until it hurts, there can be no more hurt, only more love."

— Mother Teresa

"When you wake up, the world will wake up."
Isaac Allen, Leap! Ventures LLC

Life as a documentary filmmaker, writer, and seminar leader has enabled Isaac Allen to live from inspiration and create positive material to share with the world. In 2006, Isaac experienced a divine intervention while driving home from an unethical corporation. A sense of peace swept over him and he began an odyssey that led him to discover the similarities among faiths, one common theme being that our world is an illusion. While coaching a leadership program, he met Chad Cameron, who became his co-creator on the movie, *Leap!* In *Leap!* Isaac and Chad pose the questions, "Is our reality an illusion? If so, who or what is creating the illusion?" Currently, Isaac's attention is focused on Leap! Ventures LLC as Chad and he work on producing a live workshop series called, *Leap! Beyond Limits*, and making their next documentary about integrity in business. Isaac's ultimate challenge is taking on the joys of raising two gorgeous daughters to live a life of true power, fun, and exploration.

Q. What experiences put you on your spiritual path?
A. I began seeking the truth after several challenges coalesced—leaving an unethical company, getting a divorce, etc. I sought the truth in non-dualistic traditions of oneness such as *A Course in Miracles*, Buddhism, and the writings of several past and present people such as Arnold Patent, Dan Millman, and Joe Vitale and Hew Len. Then I met my best friend and business partner, Chad Cameron, and we began making the movie, *Leap!*

Q. How did these experiences change you?
A. At first, I resisted change and, like Jonah and the big fish, the skin suit known as Isaac Allen suffered. It felt like bandages

SEEK THE LOVER WITHIN

were being ripped off my body, tearing me into shreds. But, as Joseph Campbell writes, "We must be willing to get rid of the life we've planned, so as to have the life that is waiting for us." So where the bandages had been, light started shining through and I was flooded with joy.

Q. What has been the most challenging part of your path?
A. My divorce. I thought with my background in personal development and coaching, I could make my marriage work. Eventually, I had to give up that possibility. Losing my idea of a family, my girls, was difficult. In the end, Divinity will give me what I need.

Q. What changes are you noticing about your life and the world?
A. Nothing is different and everything is different. I operate from a level of bliss that exists no matter what happens. I get to work with Chad, my brother from another mother, interviewing spiritual people committed to waking up from the dream. I spend time with my two beautiful girls.

Q. What changes are others noticing about you?
A. People say I am very business driven for a spiritual guy. Chad and I already are working on three other movies: *Handshake: Integrity in Business*; *MPower: Empowering Women in Business and Beyond*; and *Spiritual Parenting*. Chad and I still swear, joke around, and look at women. It's like the saying, "Before enlightenment, chop wood, carry water; after enlightenment, chop wood, carry water." The only person to wake up is me. I'm the one who notices that life gets more fun as I change inside.

Q. What is your earliest memory? Why do you remember it?
A. At age four, I remember my brother Mark and I playing with Tonka trucks in the doorway. We were happy and carefree as we zoomed around in our underwear. People often say children are closer to divine truth. This is because they play. When we are forty, we think there is something to do but

LESSONS FROM 50 SPIRITUAL LEADERS (VOL.1)

there is never anything but play.

A. Who are your mentors? What have you learned from them?
A. Chad Cameron, my business partner and best friend, who has such integrity. My father, who was always one hundred percent present and fun loving with us as children. Dan Millman, whose book, *Way of the Peaceful Warrior*, helped me chart a meaningful life at age eighteen. Modern day mentors include the teachings of *A Course in Miracles* and the writings of Arnold Patent and Jed McKenna.

Q. What is the greatest challenge facing society?
A. To wake up from the dream. We must wake up and realize we are one with Divinity. If we're unwilling to wake up, then whatever spiritual path we are on is just another level of the game. The newsmakers would have us believe that all these problems exist when we're actually experiencing greater peace. For example, when we are on the brink of disaster, a solution comes out of nowhere and saves us. Right now, my friend is developing a solution to end global warming.

Q. What advice would you give someone just starting his or her spiritual path?
A. Seek your truth and don't be afraid of it. Keeping leaping past illusion into what Buddhists call the void. Never delude yourself into thinking you are fully awake because it is a sure sign you are caught in ego. As Richard Bach and Jed McKenna say, "The fact that you're still alive shows there's farther to go." Watch the film, *The Truman Show*. In it, you'll see our struggle to wake up from the dream and cross the bridge into truth.

Q. What are your practices for connecting to your higher purpose?
A. There are many practices to awaken from the dream. I use Arnold Patent's mantra, "All that I see is me." I also use Hew Len's and Joe Vitale's Ho'oponopono phrase: "I love you, I'm

sorry, please forgive me, thank you." Whatever the tool, I am one hundred percent responsible for all I experience—good and bad. Being one hundred percent responsible awakens me from the dream and resolves problems because whatever is needed just shows up.

Q. How do you use these practices when you get out of balance?

A. We live in a world where people want everything to be perfect. So we put artificial laws in place, which stop life experience. I accept that I am going to get involved in conflict and drama. After Chad and I argue, we apologize, let it go, and ask, "Who's more attached to this?" Whoever's more attached wins. Then we move on without resentment.

Q. How do you balance planning with remaining open to opportunity?

A. I live my life from inspiration, from being in spirit. Inspiration is the only planning tool I need. I recently heard a minister talk about the "Footprints in the Sand" poem saying, "Go ahead and plan but write it in pencil because God ultimately will guide you. Our making *Leap!* was like the movie *Field of Dreams*. We built it and they came. When you live in spirit, life is fun. When you resist, it's not.

Q. If you received $100,000, how would you spend it?

A. I'd go to the races and spend it on ponies. Just kidding. When someone gives me $100,000, I'll see what Divinity tells me to do in the moment.

Q. If you had thirty seconds with someone in an elevator, what three things would you tell the person to do to be joyful, peaceful, and whole?

A. Operate from inspiration, letting go of judgment. Watch the movie *Leap!* Be one hundred percent present and appreciate everything.

LEAP! VENTURES, LLC

Q. What books or resources have helped you the most? Why?

A. It depends on who you are and where you are. Find the formula that works for you. It could be YouTube, meditation, and some combination of these books and movies.

Books

The Journey, by Arnold Patent

Spiritually Incorrect Enlightenment, by Jed McKenna

Zero Limits, by Joe Vitale with Dr. Hew Len

A Course in Miracles, by Helen Shucman and William Thetford

The Disappearance of the Universe, by Gary Renard

Way of the Peaceful Warrior, by Dan Millman

Surprised by Grace, by Amber Terrell

Movies and TV

Star Trek, Star Wars, The 13th Floor, The Legend of Bagger Vance, The Matrix, The Truman Show, and *The Twilight Zone*.

Q. What would you like to be written on your tombstone?

A. Nothing. When I die, my video game is over. The game is now. I am present now.

Q. Anything else?

A. Oneness means oneness—period. Being one hundred percent responsible for everything—every flower that blooms, every rape that happens, etc. If you want to wake up, you have to be one hundred percent responsible. For thousands of years, people have been talking about oneness and where is it? When you wake up, the world will wake up and you'll experience oneness. Until then, you're playing the game of illusion—separateness—with God up there and you down here.

Isaac Allen

*"A bodhisattva is someone who has com-
passion within himself or herself and who
is able to make another person smile or
help someone suffer less.
Every one of us is capable of this."*
                            - Thich Nhat Hanh

———————————————————————

Reprinted from Be Free Where You Are (2000) by Thich Nhat Hanh with permission of Parallax Press, Berkeley, California. www.parallax.org.

3

"The world is as you are."
Janet Attwood, Speaker and Best Selling Author
of *The Passion Test*

Janet Attwood is a visionary, a transformational leader, and a world humanitarian. She travels the globe, supporting people in all walks of life in knowing their personal greatness. Janet is the coauthor of the *New York Times* bestseller, *The Passion Test™— The Effortless Path to Discovering Your Life's Purpose.* She and her coauthor, Chris Attwood, have trained over 450 Passion Test Facilitators around the world (www.thepassiontest.com/cert). Jack Canfield, cocreator of the *Chicken Soup for the Soul* series and teacher in the movie, *The Secret*, has praised *The Passion Test* for providing incredible insights within a simple and easy format.

Janet has given The Passion Test™ to millions of people all over the world and has shared the same stage with top transformational leaders such as His Holiness the Dalai Lama. She is cofounder of Healthy WealthynWise Magazine (www.healthy-wealthynwise.com) and hosts the HWnW "Passion Series" in which she interviews people at the top of their field on what it takes to live a passionate life.

Through The Passion Test™, Janet and Chris Attwood have launched programs for each of these different areas: The Passion Test™ for Business, The Passion Test™ for Coaches, The Passion Test™ for Kids, The Passion Test™ for Teens, The Reclaim Your Power Program for the Homeless, and The Empowered Teen Series for kids in lockdown detention centers. For her ongoing work with homeless women and youth in lockdown detention centers, Janet received the highest award for volunteer service in the U.S. from the President of the United States—The President's Volunteer Service Award. To learn more go to: www.

thepassiontest.com or www.janetattwood.com.

Q. What experiences put you on your spiritual path?

A. I have always been drawn to spirituality and yet, I wasn't always living a spiritual life. In my teens, I was strung out on drugs. I took so much LSD that if they had given me a brain scan, it would have come out paisley! I was taking psychedelics because I thought they were my path to enlightenment. After a year of taking them, I realized they were my path to nowhere. During that time I was living in a commune, and someone walked into the commune holding an album with an Indian man on the cover. When I looked at the cover, I knew that that Indian man and I would someday meet. The Indian man was Maharishi Mahesh Yogi, the founder of the Transcendental Meditation Program, otherwise known simply as TM. Not long after I saw Maharishi's picture I stopped taking drugs and learned how to meditate, and that really was the beginning of the best part of my life.

Q. How did these experiences change you?

A. Seeing a master will change anyone because there is so much wisdom, silence, and inner happiness emanating from them. Of course, real change comes from within. So when I learned how to meditate, I became more healthy, peaceful, and centered. This is because what happens in meditation is that you gain a deep state of rest. Research has shown that what we all need in order to enjoy life is to be rested, to be less stressed. Research has also found that the only thing that releases stress is deep rest. This stress colors your existence. When you release the stress through meditation, you start to see the world as it really is, which is an incredibly abundant and beautiful world.

Q. What has been the most challenging part of your path?

A. The most challenging time was when I was taking drugs. When I stopped taking drugs and started mediating, life became a lot more effortless. The world is as you are. If you are disconnected from yourself, then you're disconnected from the rest of the world. This shows up in all kinds of ways. When you don't see the world clearly, you don't make good decisions. When you don't make good decisions, your life suffers.

Q. What is your earliest memory? Why do you remember it?

A. I remember my dad bringing home an old man named Wick who lived by himself and was very lonesome. I appreciated so much that my dad had enough love in him to recognize that this man needed a family—and for creating a family for him within our own. I also remember my dad inviting the kids down the street over for breakfast on Sundays. My two best friends were sisters named Patsy and Kathy. Their mom used to beat them daily. They had a really miserable life. My dad knew about their mom beating them and he always made sure that Patsy and Kathy spent their Sunday mornings with us. I love how my dad noticed what they needed and gave that loving kindness to them. It was the same with my mom. It was those memories that shaped me and served as reminders of how to be in the world.

Q. Who are your mentors? What have you learned from them?

A. Maharishi Mahesh Yogi has always been my first and most important teacher. His effortless technique of Transcendental Meditation has been a process that I use every single day. Byron Katie is my other great mentor. I love her process called "The Work" because it gets rid of any limiting beliefs we have. Through her work, Katie shows us that the only thing that gets in the way of anyone being present in the moment and "loving what is" is their false beliefs. These false beliefs cause us to view others and ourselves in ways that are out of touch with reality and cause us pain, separation, and suffering. Whenever I become aware that I'm unhappy about a person, situation or thing, I use Katie's process to turn those thoughts around so I can see that the story I was telling myself was worse than the reality.

JANET ATTWOOD

Katie says that every moment is a gift and the only things that get in the way of any of us being able to see life as this great gift are our false beliefs, false ideas, and false concepts. Therefore, when anything brings you pain and/or separation, if you use this simple process of self-inquiry, you will be able to turn those thoughts around and, again, see that the gift was always there.

One of my passions was to travel the world interviewing the greatest masters in the world. In the last five years, I have interviewed around one hundred masters. I would definitely say that Byron Katie is as awake as the most enlightened masters. For any Master Trainer of my Passion Test Certification Program, it is a prerequisite for all of them to go to Katie's school for The Work.

Q. What is the greatest challenge facing society?
A. Ignorance of our divine nature and belief in the idea that we are separate from one another, that we exist in isolation. When we believe that we are separate, then everything becomes mirrored by this reality. It becomes an "all about me" world. Problems in society arise simply because people do not know that at our very core, we are all unified. Quantum physics talks about this unified field that underlies all of creation and that we are all parcel and part of this unified field.

When we believe we are "separate," then we come from a consciousness of lack and limitation and it shows up in all kinds of ways that do not promote healthy living for the individual and for society. Maharishi has a great answer to the world's problems—meditate to raise the consciousness of society. The collective practice of meditating together two times a day not only raises the consciousness of the people meditating, but research from Yale, Harvard, Stanford, and other top colleges suggests that it also raises the collective consciousness of society.

Q. If you had thirty seconds with someone in an elevator, what three things would you tell him or her to do to be joyful, peaceful, and whole?

A. First thing I would tell them is to learn how to meditate. Life is here to enjoy. The simple practice of meditating twice a day gives an individual a deep state of rest, and from that rested state all kinds of wonderful things start to occur. On the level of the mind, when the mind is clear, people start to "do less and accomplish more." When an individual is more rested, the body is refreshed, they have more energy, more vitality. When there is more energy, people become happier. When people become happier, they are more loving to others. It sets off a wonderful chain of positive events.

The second thing I would tell them to do is use Byron Katie's simple process called, "The Work" to get rid of any limiting beliefs. And the last thing I would tell them to do is take The Passion Test™ and then choose in favor of their passions. The secret to living a passionate life is simply that whenever you are faced with a choice, a decision, or an opportunity, choose in favor of your passions.

Q. How would you respond to those who say it's more important to love others than yourself; that the true path to loving yourself is through loving others first?

A. How can you love anyone if you don't love yourself? Is it easy to love humanity when you feel disconnected? For me, the answer is never. All love is connected to the self. I meet no one but me. That's my experience. When I am connected, then it's effortless to love. When I am not connected, then how can I feel anything? From fullness comes fullness. It's that simple. Gandhi said it best when he said, "Be the change you wish to see in the world."

Q. How do you balance planning with remaining open to opportunity?

JANET ATTWOOD

A. I spoke at an event with the Dalai Lama last week. For events like these, I have to plan. However, if I drive to the airport and miss my flight, then I know I'm not supposed to get on it. So I make plans and then let go. I surrender, knowing that every moment is going to deliver exactly what I need.

Q. What books or resources have helped you the most? Why?
A. *The Science of Being and Art of Living*, Maharishi Mahesh Yogi
Loving What Is: Four Questions that Can Change Your Life, by Byron Katie
The Speed of Trust, by Stephen Covey
The Soul of Money: Transforming Your Relationship with Money and Life, by Lynne Twist

I also, of course, recommend the *The Passion Test™—The Effortless Path to Discovering Your Life Purpose*, by Chris Attwood and me. *The Passion Test™* is great for helping people align with their passions, which are the clues to their destiny, their purpose. All of us have a desire to give, but we can only give from what we have. *The Passion Test™* gets people clear on what they care about most. When they connect with that, then life becomes a divine experience of effortless giving.

Q. What would you like to be written on your tombstone?
A. That I lived a passionately happy, committed life in service to humanity.

"Gratitude is the single best way to connect with God."
Bob Burg, Speaker and Best Selling Author

Bob Burg is a highly sought after speaker at corporate, financial services, and direct sales conventions. Combining humor and entertainment with easily applied, proven systems for personal marketing, audiences come away ready to immediately profit from Bob's instruction. Relating the principles contained in his best selling books, Bob has addressed audiences ranging from fifty to 16,000 people, sharing the platform with notables including top thought leaders, broadcast personalities, athletes, and even a former U.S. President. His critically acclaimed book, *Endless Referrals: Network Your Everyday Contacts Into Sales*, has sold over 175,000 copies and is used as a training manual for top sales organizations throughout the world. His latest national bestseller, *The Go-Giver*, coauthored with John David Mann, has been heralded as a new business classic, selling over 100,000 copies in just its first year. Bob is an advocate for the free enterprise system and seeks to empower individuals and organizations to thrive and grow by putting its principles to work. He puts his go-giver abilities to use for charities, being a former Palm Beach County/Brooks Brothers Leukemia Society Man of the Year for his fundraising efforts and a former Board Member of Safe Harbor, the Humane Society of Jupiter, Florida.

Q. What experiences put you on your spiritual path?
A. It is important to define the word "spiritual." As Don Miguel Ruiz writes in *The Four Agreements*, we perceive the world a certain way and assume everyone else sees it as we do. That's why when Jesse Ventura, then Governor of Minnesota said, "Organized religion is a sham and a crutch for weak-minded people . . . " a well-known theologian repeated this phrase as though Ventura had said *faith* is a sham. Ventura

had not said that. However, because this person's sense of faith was so intertwined with his religion, he could not differentiate between the two terms. My father's strong faith, deeply rooted in Judaism, put me on a spiritual path early. I see God as a universal benevolent presence that guides us all. Like my dad, I honor whatever path an individual chooses to take that leads to God and connects to Spirit.

Q. How did these experiences change you?
A. My dad taught me early on that God has a reason for everything. I have greater piece of mind knowing that everything happens for a reason, even if I don't know what that reason is. I do know my purpose and that is to follow God's will, as I believe it to be. However, during difficult times, I still struggle asking, "Why me?" Then, I think, *Why not me?* Since humans cannot reason as well as our creator, I try and remain patient—knowing it's all in God's hands. Fortunately, the good times in life far outweigh the bad.

Q. What changes are you noticing about your life and the world?
A. I look at what tyrannical governments do to people and I take it personally. With all our knowledge, wisdom, and technology, most people still live under the rule of thugs. This situation wouldn't bother me so much if I could see from a higher consciousness and remain aware but detached. I try, but I'm not there yet. I'm like John Denver's character in the movie, *Oh, God!* in which God, played by George Burns, tells him something like, "Trust me. In the end, you'll see." I gain solace believing that someday the reason for everything will be revealed. I'd like to know it while I'm here on Earth but I don't see that happening.

Q. What changes are others noticing about you?
A. I have become calmer as I get older and continue to grow. My mind used to race a million miles a minute and it was obvious to everyone around me. Now, it's not so obvious as I develop a more peaceful presence.

AUTHOR/SPEAKER

Q. What has been the most challenging part of your path?

A. I suffer from obsessive-compulsive disorder (OCD), a chemi-cal imbalance of the brain. I have experienced OCD since I was a child, but it hit full force in my late teens. Fortunately, in my twenties I found a doctor familiar with OCD and was able to begin getting help. It's difficult to be thankful to God for giving me OCD because I have had to succeed in spite of it. However, it has certainly made me a more empathetic person, able to identify with the pain of others. People say that after talking with me, they feel understood. Perhaps that's part of my purpose here on Earth.

Q. What is your earliest memory? Why do you remember it?

A. I have a lot of childhood memories, so I am not certain which is the earliest. I do remember feeling I was destined to make a difference. I just didn't know how. I thought I could become Batman, but forgot this aspiration when the show went off the air. Later in life, I met Yvonne Craig, who played Batgirl, and helped her a bit with her book, *From Ballet to the Bat-cave and Beyond*. She was very sweet and thanked me in the acknowledgements. That's the closest I came to being Batman.

Q. Who are your mentors? What have you learned from them?

A. My main mentors are my parents, who taught me how to live life by way of their love and wonderful example. I recently gave a talk in Rhode Island that my cousin and her husband attended. Afterwards, she came up to me and exclaimed, "Bob, it's unbelievable. Hearing you speak is just like listen-ing to Uncle Sumner (my dad)." That's the nicest compliment I could ever receive. I often feel as though I'm taking my dad's message and sharing it with a wider audience through books such as *The Go-Giver*. For example, it's interesting that many people believe you can either be nice or finish first. However, the vast majority of successful people have enormous integ-rity, which contributed to their achievements. My dad is one

BOB BURG

such example. My mission is to teach people that the more they give through adding value to others, the more they will prosper. I have had other mentors who come at just the right time to help me in specific areas. As the Talmud says, "Who is wise? One who learns from all people."

Q. What is the greatest challenge facing society?

A. We have been sliding into socialism for the past seventy-five years. Every country that has embraced it has experienced poverty, corruption, and violence. Socialism's grand ideas always blow up just like those of Tim Allen's character on the television show *Home Improvement*. With true free enterprise comes unlimited opportunity for those who want it, and plenty of charity for those who need it. People say they want free enterprise but still clamor for more government. Despite this incongruity, I'm optimistic that worldwide socialism won't happen. Still, sometimes I fear we're like the story of the frog getting boiled so slowly he doesn't realize the need to jump out until it's too late.

Q. What advice would you give someone just starting his or her spiritual path?

A. I would first ask the person to define what he or she means by "spirituality." If the person followed a particular organized religion, I would advise him or her to find a good church, synagogue, mosque, or temple. If the individual's faith were a different type of connection to God, then I would encourage him or her to find books that resonate and provide strength. I would also, if asked, share what God, the ultimate source of everything, means to me.

Q. What are your practices for connecting to your higher purpose?

A. When I awake in the morning, I thank God for bringing me back to life and say a Jewish prayer, the *Shema*. I say the *Shema* again at night when I go to bed. During the day, I do my best to remain conscious of God and live life accordingly. The

Author/Speaker

more conscious I am, the stronger my connection to God is.

Q. How do you use these practices when you get out of balance?

A. I return to consciousness by asking, "Is this really a big deal?" It's usually not. In his book, *The Science Of Getting Rich*, Wallace D. Wattles has a whole chapter on gratitude. Gratitude is the single best way to remain connected to the source of all. For example, the first line of my morning prayer is, "I express my gratitude to You, the King who is alive and always exists for returning my soul to me with compassion." In Yogi Berra style, I would say, "We need to stay conscious to be conscious."

Q. How do you balance planning with remaining open to opportunity?

A. While I set goals, I try and stay conscious of not being attached to specific results. I believe this is the best way to remain open to other opportunities that come along.

Q. If you received $100,000, how would you spend it?

A. Being a capitalist, I would expect to have earned it by first providing value. But whether through that or the proverbial winning of the lottery, I would accept the money and then give some away. I would give ten percent to Safe Harbor, the Humane Society of Jupiter, Florida, where I was a board member. I'd give another ten percent to other causes I support and then invest the remainder. I'm not a stuff person, so there isn't anything I really need. I've gone and done most of what I want to do.

Q. If you had thirty seconds with someone in an elevator, what three things would you tell the person to do to be joyful, peaceful, and whole?

A. I would first ask, "Do you really want to be joyful?" Sometimes people say they do and then come up with excuses for being miserable. If the person truly did, then I'd advise her

BOB BURG

to act as if she already is joyful, etc. The mind cannot hold two opposing thoughts—the act of smiling and the feeling of sadness. The sadness has to go because, when we change our physicality, we change our feelings. So act your way into joy by smiling, walking tall, and moving with energy and purpose.

Q. What books or resources have helped you the most? Why?

A. I like reading because I enjoy time alone to study and reflect. I especially like personal development classics such as:
How to Win Friends and Influence People, by Dale Carnegie
Think and Grow Rich, by Napoleon Hill
As A Man Thinketh, by James Allen
The Science Of Getting Rich, by Wallace D. Wattles
Peace, Power & Plenty, by Orison Swett Marden
The Autobiography of Benjamin Franklin, by Benjamin Franklin
The Four Agreements, by Don Miguel Ruiz
Psycho-Cybernetics, by Maxwell Maltz

Sometimes just a few lines of a book can change a life. Here are some examples:
In *The Celestine Prophecy*, James Redfield writes that everyone has a personal drama. By identifying my dramas and those of others, I gradually lessened their effect on me.
In *The Road Less Traveled*, M. Scott Peck's first paragraph says, "Life is difficult . . . once we truly understand and accept it . . . then life is no longer difficult." This one insight alone has helped me effectively deal with many of life's challenges.
In *Psycho-Cybernetics*, Maxwell Maltz says we have an ". . . automatic guidance system . . .[like] a self-aiming torpedo or missile . . ." that is programmed to succeed (or fail) in specific areas of our lives. What a great lesson: change your program and you can change your life.

Q. What would you like to be written on your tombstone?

AUTHOR/SPEAKER

A. "He made people feel good about themselves." Doing this feels very natural to me and is another one of those traits I learned from emulating my dad. I believe that making people feel genuinely good about themselves is one of the greatest mitzvahs (good deeds) someone can do. Hopefully, I do this enough. I'm never sure.

Q. Anything else?

A. Keep your mind open, but not so open that you forgo your principles. Learn from everyone. However, as author and speaker Jim Rohn says, "From some people you learn what to do, and from others you learn what not to do." When you find yourself resisting new information, question your premises. Ask, "Am I resisting this experience based on sound logic, or an outdated belief that needs to change?" This type of self-examination will keep you growing.

Bob Burg

"If God is everywhere, he is in you. If he is in you, then you are everywhere."
- Deepak Chopra

_____

"The world is nothing more or less than the consciousness I use to see it."
Alan Cohen, Best Selling Author and Founder of All About U

Alan Cohen, M.A., is the author of twenty-two popular inspirational books and CDs, including the best-selling *The Dragon Doesn't Live Here Anymore*, the award winning *A Deep Breath of Life*, and the classic *Are You as Happy as Your Dog?* He is a contributing writer for *The New York Times* number one best selling series *Chicken Soup for the Soul*, and his books have been translated into twenty-three foreign languages. His work has been featured on Oprah.com and in *101 Top Experts*. Alan's monthly column, *From the Heart*, appears in magazines internationally, along with his interviews.

Alan is a respected keynoter and seminar leader for professional meetings in the fields of personal growth, inspiration, holistic health, human relations, and achievement of work/life balance. He conducts Life Mastery Trainings around the world and is the founder of All About U, a university without walls dedicated to higher learning for the higher self. Alan is a faculty member of Omega Institute for Holistic Studies, and appears regularly on national radio and television.

Alan brings a warm blend of wisdom, intimacy, humor, and vision to the path of personal, professional, and spiritual growth. He loves to extract lessons from the practical experiences of daily living and find beauty in the seemingly mundane. Many readers and seminar participants have reported that his teachings have brought them deep encouragement and empowerment, and inspired them to believe in themselves and achieve new levels of success in their personal and professional lives.

ALAN COHEN

Q. What experiences put you on your spiritual path

A. Pretty much all of them because everything is for learning, isn't it? I have had a number of particular turnabout points. I remember being in college and living very much in my head. I was searching, wondering, and feeling lost and disconnected. Then I went to a human relations retreat where we had a dozen people in a cabin in the woods relating to each other for a weekend. During that time, I realized I had been disconnected from my heart, my truth. I began trusting my feelings, speaking my truth, and letting others in. I realized there was so much more to life than I was allowing at the moment. I set out to study with every guru, mentor, guide, and shaman I could to help discover who I really was—in spite of who I had been told I was. So that's one piece of it. I also have had many relationship ups and downs. Life is a spiritual path.

> "What we are looking for, we already are."

Q. How did these experiences change you?

A. I felt freer and lighter. I trusted more. When I was in Bali in the early 1990s, I lost ten pounds in two weeks. And it was not like I was really overweight, but I had just lightened up. I realized that when I lightened up spiritually, I also lightened up physically without even trying. The bottom line is that I just felt more connected to others, the universe, and life. I discovered that God was in my heart, not sitting on a distant cloud somewhere.

Q. What has been the most challenging part of your path?

A. My mind. If I look back, I would say that self-doubt has been my biggest enemy. I notice there were a number of things I could or would have done but, at the time, I didn't believe in myself. I also notice that the times I did succeed and grow were those when I honored my inner voice and trusted its guidance. The more I doubted myself, the worse I felt and the less I succeeded. And the more I trusted myself, the more I succeeded. The rational mind can get between true self and life. After mediating for many years, I still have to work daily at keeping a childlike mind, opening to spirit, and just staying in the flow rather than overthinking things.

Q. You mention your mind has gotten in the way. Has your mind also helped you?

A. The rational mind is a fabulous servant but a lousy master. It is really good when you are balancing your checkbook, measuring your rug, or planning your vacation. It is not so good when you are looking at relationships and God. We have developed the rational mind in Western culture to the nth degree. At its best, it can illuminate the more subtle aspects of how God works. There is a whole yoga called Gyan yoga that is based on using the mind to recognize God and to actually go beyond the mind. But most people don't use the mind to recognize God. They use the mind to deny God. So it is probably safe to say that for most in our culture, the more we move beyond our thoughts, the closer we come to the truth.

Q. What is your earliest memory? Why do you remember it?

A. I must have been five years old and we had a parakeet named Petey Boy. He was my pet and he lived on a little table next to my bed. He would come into my bed and jump around and play with me. I remember waking up one morning and playing with him for the longest time, just feeling happy. To me, that memory symbolizes a childlike innocence where I had not learned to think so hard yet and was just enjoying being with a natural spirit in the form of a parakeet. Now, many years later, I have five dogs and I am doing the same thing with them. It's just that connection with innocence and natural knowing.

> "I discovered that God was in my heart, not sitting on a distant cloud somewhere."

ALAN COHEN

I also had some mystical experiences. One was a dream where I was looking under my bed and there were images of cartoon characters around that were all lit up. The content of the dream was uninteresting but the feeling of it was mystical. It was almost as if that was my first vision of God. It was as if these characters that were joyful to me had become windows of the divine. I felt like I was lifted out of the Earth plane and into some higher states of awareness with that childlike venue.

Q. You seem to have a talent for making mystical principles relevant to everyday life. Please tell me more about this area.

A. That is one of the aspects of my teaching that I receive the most feedback on. I bring metaphysical principles to Earthly experiences. I don't know if I even try to do that. It's just the way I think about life. I try to look for God in the flow of daily life. You are coming to a very important point here and I know you will really emphasis this in your book. The world is not separate from God. It is not some penal colony for people who didn't make the cut, as some would have us believe. It's really an expression of God and all the lessons of God are available on Earth. In fact, it's a wonderful training ground

> **"Nature is my church."**

to discover God. For example, if you don't use the upset you had with your spouse for learning, you missed the whole point of being here. It's not about getting somewhere; it's about milking the lessons that are right here.

Q. Who are your mentors? What have you learned from them?

A. I studied for many years with an amazing spiritual master. Her name was Hilda Charlton and she lived in New York. She was a self-styled master, an American who had lived in India for many years and had done spiritual practices there. She came back to the United States during the 1960s when there was an explosion of consciousness. Lots of people who were

ALL ABOUT U

looking for healing and higher awareness found her. She spent her life giving love, healing, doing psychic work, channeling, blessing, and teaching people. I studied with her very closely for fourteen years. She had integrity of the highest degree and gave me an impeccable foundation. I was very fortunate to have studied with her.

Q. What is the greatest challenge facing society?

A. One is fear. People don't trust that life is working on their behalf and then they make decisions out of fear and desperation, which just get them into more trouble. But then it's also learning, so eventually you figure it out and retrace your steps. But wouldn't it be nice if we had fewer steps to retrace? On a deeper level, it's lack of self-awareness, lack of identity with Spirit. People feel disconnected from life, from their hearts, from God and the universe. There is tremendous loneliness out there with people running, running, running. They are shopping and buying and striving to get on *Oprah*. Striving to do all kinds of things on the outside world that basically deny they are enough as they are. If we could just realize that we already have and are what we seek. Finding the right lover, getting on *Oprah*, or making a business coup, those are all fine pursuits, but we need to hold them lightly as we recognize that what we are looking for, we already are. If we can just get that, everything shifts and we start living from overflow rather than lack or need.

Q. If you had thirty seconds with someone in an elevator, what three things would you tell him or her to do to be joyful, peaceful, and whole?

A. Trust their intuition, follow their hearts, and recognize that truth lives inside them. The whole game of life is not about seeking. It's more about finding and allowing. When I work with people in coaching, I usually invite them to discover where their passion lives and tell the truth about it. The problem with most people is not that they lack passion. The problem is that they are not in touch with the passion they

ALAN COHEN

already have. So I invite people to align with where their inner self is moving them, and to believe that God is trying to work through them, not against them. Once people start to trust their inner knowing, they become their own master and they don't need to come to me or anyone else for advice because that voice of the divine is speaking to them fully in their own heart.

Q. What are your practices for connecting to your higher purpose?

A. I meditate every morning for twenty to forty minutes. I do *A Course in Miracles* lesson. I've been doing that for many, many years and it keeps going deeper. I do some yoga. I get outside as much as I can. I love to walk in nature. Nature is my church. When I get to the beach or the forest, I feel very much in God's presence. I watch movies and play with my partner, Dee. We have a great relationship. We do a lot of connecting over fun things in our family and with our dogs. All these things contribute to my well-being and to my way of staying connected.

Q. How do you use these practices when you get out of balance?

A. I do have those moments. More than I would care to admit or more than most people realize—connected, disconnected, connected, disconnected. In the long run, I am more connected than disconnected. Sometimes a money issue will come up or sometimes I'll have an argument with my partner. I try to bring myself back to consciousness by mediating, doing yoga, or reading *A Course in Miracles*. I do a lot of reframing. For example, I asked someone for a favor the other day regarding my work. It was someone I really respect and hoped would help me out. To date, the person hasn't given me a response. I felt disappointed and angry. So I said, "I know anger is an illusion that is based on a lie I tell myself. I am believing that my happiness, success, and well-being depend on this person. And in this moment, they have not

ALL ABOUT U

offered it. Is it really true that I need them for this project?"

As I began to scan my field of options, the truth was that they might not be needed for this project. I reasoned out that this person was not the source of my good—that the universe, God, abundance, truth, nature, whatever you want to call it, is. My good is flowing to me through many angles beyond which I can figure out myself. In fact, two other wonderful people showed up and offered me what this other person wasn't offering me at the moment. I felt deeply touched that these people said, "Yes, I will help you." So God was in charge of the game, not me. And when I realized that, I felt a sense of relief and peace.

> "Everything you see out there is a result of your own thoughts. So change those thoughts and everything you see will change."

Q. How do you balance planning with remaining open to opportunity?

A. The more I mature spiritually, the less I plan. *A Course in Miracles* says that the healed mind does not plan. That confronts us because we spend a lot of time planning. I don't think it means we should never plan because if I'm going to get on a plane, I might want to make a reservation before showing up at the airport. So a certain amount of life requires planning. The *Course* is talking more about fearful planning—if I don't do this, then something bad will happen—or planning as a substitute for being.

My best days are the ones when I don't have a major agenda and just move with the energy. If I feel like writing, playing with the dog, or going into town for lunch, I just do it. I have these days more and more. It's like when you go to the department store and you step in front of the electronic sensor and the doors open automatically. I have entire days like this where I go from one cool thing to the next and everything seems to flow. I enjoy those days much more than the ones I plan out. There is a magical element that I don't find when I over plan.

Q. If you received $100,000, how would you spend it?

A. I feel like I have already won the lotto. Not just financially. I have a wonderful partner, dogs, friends, and home. There is a house we have our eye on that is really expansive and beautiful. So if we hit the jackpot that would be the first thing we would do. There are organizations that I would help. My partner and I already help them with what we have, but we also make lists of others we would help with more resources. We fantasize about bringing kids from the inner city to Hawaii. We're also animal lovers and there are certain animal sanctuaries we would support.

We do this fun exercise called *The Prosperity Game* that Abraham teaches. You make an imaginary bank account and put in a thousand dollars on day one, two thousand dollars on day two, and so forth. Then you write imaginary checks to things you would use the money for. You do this for thirty days and by the end, you have lots of money to play with. Dee and I decided to do this with millions instead of thousands. At first, we spent it on ourselves—things we wanted. Then we started spending more on charity. After the fifteenth day, I realized we were giving away millions of dollars and that the money wasn't going to solve the world's problems. Consciousness, not money, is going to do that. If we can contribute to up-leveling the consciousness of the planet, then that would be a major step toward solving society's ills. That was an interesting exercise—to go to the end of what money can do and then see what was beyond that.

Q. What are your specific experiences around up-leveling consciousness?

A. It's the best question because the answer goes the deepest. My purpose in life, besides sheer joy, is to up-level my consciousness. The world that I see out there is nothing more or less than the consciousness I am using to see it. When I recognize the presence of God in that moment, I am upgrading not just *my* consciousness, but also the consciousness of the planet. When we pray for people or send love or mediate, what we are doing is learning to look at life through the eyes of God. And God does not see lack, pain, fear, starvation, hunger, or loss of any kind. God consciousness is simple wholeness, oneness, and joy.

Two things happen when I come from the perspective of oneness. First, I feel better because I am lined up with my natural knowing and can see life as it is. Second—and here's the fun part—events, people, and experiences actually shift as my consciousness does. That's the miracle factor because we do not know exactly how that works. But, as Wayne Dyer says, ". . . change the way you see the world and the world you see will change." It does not change because you think it does; it changes because you thought it did and then actual events manifested around that. So up-leveling my consciousness is my gift to the planet, which flows to everyone I think about, see, touch, and know.

Q. What books or resources have helped you the most? Why?
A. *A Course in Miracles* has been, in some ways, the best teaching I have ever had. It's all about healing the mind, loving, forgiving and allowing God to being present. So I always recommend the *Course*, not that it's for everybody, but if people get into it, it will definitely change their lives. Abraham-Hicks is very powerful. I have benefited a lot from this material. I also have discovered a fellow who is doing some very interesting work named Dr. Ihaleakala Hew Len. He tells how he used this Hawaiian healing method called Ho'oponopono to transform a ward of the criminally insane to which he was assigned as a psychologist. His whole teaching is that every-

ALAN COHEN

thing you see out there is a result of your own thoughts. So change those thoughts and everything you see will change. I've been enjoying his work and I met him and appreciated him in person. So those are three resources that I think people can't go wrong with.

Q. Anything else?

A. I have a new book called, *A Daily Dose of Sanity*. It has a five-minute reading for each day that will uplift, inspire, and guide you. That is symbolic of what we need on the planet right now. This is a very holy and fertile time. We certainly have our share of challenges, but with each challenge comes opportunity. I invite people to reframe what seems to be going on in the outer world into a spiritual opportunity.

We are coming into a period of phenomenal abundance, not just materially but also spiritually. If we can just reframe events to reflect that, we're in for a terrific ride.

All About U

"I am living the Gospel a new way."
Sister Annie Credidio, Founder of Damien House

Sister Annie Credidio, Sisters of Charity of the Blessed Virgin Mary (B.V.M.), has dedicated her life to bringing care and dignity to Hansen's patients. In the late 1980s, Annie began volunteering in the Hansen's wing of one of Santiago de Guayaquil, Ecuador's hospitals, teaching arts and crafts to the patients. As she formed relationships with the staff and residents, she realized she and the hospital could do much more to dispel the misery in these patients' lives. In the early 1990s, Sister Annie and other hospital volunteers reorganized the Hansen's (leprosy) wing to form Damien House, hoping to transform the lives of patients with Hansen's disease. Through her vision and leadership, Damien House has restored the health, hope, and confidence of several thousand patients and their family members. In 1994, Annie founded the U.S. based Damien House charitable organization, which invites donors to join the effort to bring hope and dignity to the lives of Hansen's patients. In addition to running the hospital, Sister Annie spends several months of the year traveling in the U.S. to seek the funding that keeps Damien House open.

Q. What experiences put you on your spiritual path?

A. I grew up in Brooklyn, down the street from our Catholic church, Saint Cecilia's. When I played with the neighbor kids, I could always see the church. I loved going there because it provided a peaceful refuge away from our noisy household. I had a warm feeling about church because it was a time to gather with family and celebrate events like first communion. Also, our parents bought us candy after mass, so I liked that too.

During my teens, I went through a rebellious stage as my

family coped with illness and I questioned why I was Catholic. I left the church for two years. During that time, I felt empty so I decided to return. That was a pivotal moment for me because it was my choice to be Catholic. Afterwards, all the rituals became more meaningful. I had to leave the church in order to fully appreciate and belong to it.

In 1968, I considered joining a community of sisters when the church—due to social upheaval—put a freeze on entry into communities. So instead, I taught at a preschool for children of recent immigrants. Two nuns ran the school. They belonged to the Sisters of Charity of the Blessed Virgin Mary (B.V.M.) and were different from the nuns I'd known before. They created such a joyful, lively atmosphere for the students and teachers. And their lives so reflected the Gospel that I started to think about the possibility of becoming one of them.

A few years later, after my parents and brother died, I said to them, "I am looking for a community of sisters that is moving with the times, one that will accept me, help me grow, and allow me to learn from them as they learn from me." They suggested I look at the B.V.M.s. When I went to the mother house in Dubuque, Iowa, I felt like I was coming home. I fell in love with the sisters and their philosophy and began the long process of initiation. I knew I was called to do something in the world and that if I listened to my heart, God would lead me down the right path. I always follow my heart (the Spirit) and I've never had a sleepless night as a result.

In my early years with the community, I said I would never leave Brooklyn. Then I lived in Chicago for a couple of years and said, "I'll never leave the U.S. because there is so much need here." Then one of our sisters went down to Ecuador and invited me to join her. I went down for six weeks and fell in love the country and its people. I ended up going back and staying in Bolivia to study Spanish for a year. During that time, I met many children who had been abandoned because their parents couldn't afford them. These children, who had suffered so much, were craving love and I decided to be with them. But when I returned to Ecuador from Bolivia, my heart said I wasn't supposed to remain at the children's school. I went into deep prayer to discern what was going on.

Then someone invited me to attend liturgy at a local hospital. When I was sitting in the pew, a lady crawled on her hands and knees to greet me. She extended her hand and I saw that she had no fingers. She also had no toes, teeth, or cartilage in her nose. Her eyes were cloudy and she was partially blind. Yet, she had a warm, welcoming smile. I asked the woman who invited me, "Where are we?" She replied, "We are at a hospital for people with leprosy," what I later learned is called Hansen's disease. I looked around the chapel and saw people in different stages of the disease. They had matted hair, undressed wounds, and sadness in their hearts. Since many did not have fingers, they shook hands by touching elbows. At that moment, I realized God had called me to Ecuador to be with them. I went back to the facility several times to teach arts and crafts. While I was there, I felt such peacefulness in my heart.

After two years of doing arts and crafts with the patients, I knew there was something wrong at the hospital. But, I wasn't sure what it was since I was only there one day a week. So, with the blessings of the children's school and my community of sisters, I went to work full-time at the hospital. I started by fixing the building's infrastructure—things like pipes and sanitation. It was a spirituality of action. I was living the Gospel in a way I hadn't before. There was a happiness in my heart. Twenty-one years later, I still don't consider it work. It's my life. It's a part of me.

SISTER ANNIE CREDIDIO

Q. How did these experiences change you?

A. I look at the church as an institution in a different way. We had trouble getting priests to do the liturgy at the hospital because they were in short supply and the local parishes needed them. So we took it upon ourselves to make our own celebrations.

During this period I realized that if I had had the opportunity to be ordained in the Catholic Church, I could have done those liturgies. This experience helped me see that we are the church. We are all called to be priests, to do what we have to do to make church. When we live the Gospel on a daily basis, it becomes a part of us. Then scripture becomes so much more meaningful. We come to see that Jesus reached out to those who had so little—and that we are called to do the same. I choose to live simply so others may live.

Q. What has been the most challenging part of your path?

A. My friends and I formed a nonprofit organization called Damien House. It's a place where people infected with Hansen's disease can live and have a greater voice. Damien House is named after Father Damien de Veuster, who died of Hansen's disease and was recently canonized a saint. I named it after him because I wanted to honor his commitment to helping people with the disease. The first challenge was founding the organization once I felt sure it was what God wanted. The second—and ongoing—challenge is raising the necessary funds to keep our doors open. It was especially tough during Hurricane Katrina and the tsunami in Thailand when people had already given so much to those affected by these disasters and couldn't give any more. But our doors remain open because we constantly pray to Father Damien and he answers our prayers. Sometimes we are almost out of money and then, out of the blue, a donation will come. Father Damien's miracles have kept us afloat and ready to

DAMIEN HOUSE

serve newcomers for the past fifteen years.

Q. What is your earliest memory? Why do you remember it?

A. My little brother's baptism when I was six years old. After he was baptized, the whole family came over to the house to celebrate. I am from a large Italian family, so we had this huge tray of Italian cookies. While eating these delicious treats, I remember thinking, *Wow, this is great! This baptism has brought us all together.*

Q. Who are your mentors? What have you learned from them?

A. My grandmother, who lived to be ninety-nine-and-a-half years old, and aunts who lived next door to us and always had time for me. They taught me about perseverance and unconditional love. They didn't want anything from me, only my presence. My presence was their present! Two nuns who taught at my elementary school and were always warm and kind. Another nun who taught at my high school and listened to me when I was going through tough times. Sister Saint Joseph and Sister Lorna Colin who ran the preschool where I worked after college, as well as the two women who ran the Nuevo Mundo school in Ecuador. All these women were committed to giving children an education so they would have more choices in life.

My identical twin is also a mentor. Our unconditional love for each other is the closest I have come to knowing what God's love is like. I'm sixty years old and I have never been angry with her. Even when we were little, I could never go to bed upset with her. We'd always talk and work things out.

Q. What is the greatest challenge facing society?

A. Peace and survival. We have to learn to make peace with one another and with Mother Earth. We have to learn to live with less so more may survive. Our negative energy and mis-guided actions have taken a toll on the Earth and ourselves.

Sister Annie Credidio

Q. What advice would you give someone just starting his or her spiritual path?

A. I would tell them that there are many religions and I would encourage them to take part in different services. This would help them make an informed decision. I would also make literature available and invite them to participate in any prayers or services we had going on. In addition, I would pray for them while they were making their decision.

Q. What are your practices for connecting to your higher purpose?

A. I begin my day by reading and reflecting on the scriptures. Journaling about them helps me internalize their meaning. If I don't have this quiet time, I find myself frazzled and less patient throughout the day. When I become overwhelmed, I go into a chapel we have at the hospital and take a little time for myself.

Q. How do you use these practices when you get out of balance?

A. I grew up in an Italian family with a mother who had strong opinions. Sometimes, during a crisis, my first reaction is to think that my opinion counts more. I even have a tendency to get angry or emotional if someone disagrees with me. Then I step back, take a deep breath, and remember that everybody has a right to their opinion. My community of sisters has been instrumental in teaching me about dialogue. Their philosophy is that we need to sit down and talk with each other to resolve issues. If we can do this, then world peace becomes possible.

Q. If you received $100,000, how would you spend it?

A. Damien House's annual budget is $200,000, so that would pay for half a year of patient care. The money would be used to provide patients with medicine, wound and eye treatment, twenty-four hour care from nurse's aides, and three hot, nutritious meals a day.

Q. If you had thirty seconds with someone in an elevator, what three things would you tell him or her to do to be joyful, peaceful, and whole?

A. I hardly ever take elevators. But if I were on one, I would smile at the person. That's because when I am down, someone smiling at me always helps. The face of Christ is in everyone—like that woman infected with Hansen's disease who crawled over to me in the hospital chapel. When she smiled, I truly saw the face of Christ. So just a simple smile can ease someone's tension.

Q. What books or resources have helped you the most? Why?

A. I'm not one of those people who can rattle off the names of books. I like books that have a moral to the story, that leave me in a pensive mood. I like biographies for that reason. They help me reflect on a person's contributions and leave me with a good feeling. I also find my community's monthly reflections to be nourishing to the soul. Of course, during international travel, I'll read almost anything. In addition, I like quiet, reflective music.

Q. What would you like to be written on your tombstone?

A. "Annie was fully present in body and now she is fully present in spirit." When I am with someone, I give them my full presence. When I leave this world, I will continue to give people my full presence in spirit.

Q. Anything else?

A. I was reading an issue of the *National Catholic Reporter* that said Father Damien is the patron saint of people infected with HIV/AIDS and Hansen's disease. I thought, *Wait a minute!* Father Damien died of Hansen's disease, which is on the rise in the U.S. (6,500 cases) and other countries. But by put-

Sister Annie Credidio

ting the disease second, the journalist gave the impression that it doesn't exist anymore, that it was only a threat during the nineteenth century when Father Damien was alive.

I wish I had contacted the *National Catholic Reporter* to do a follow-up piece. In that article, I could have told people that ninety-five percent of us have a basic immunity to the disease and that people with low defenses—especially those in developing countries who lack nutrition—are susceptible. In the U.S. there are many people in treatment at hospitals with infectious disease units such as Belleview Hospital Center and the University of Illinois Medical Center. We just don't know about it due to our privacy laws. However, you can't get Hansen's disease from someone who is in treatment. The most likely way is through prolonged contact with someone who has the disease and is not in treatment. This is especially true in impoverished regions with poor sanitation. Sometimes people who have resources feel guilty and don't know how to go about sharing them. They can make a difference by giving to organizations that help the voiceless in society—the elderly, children, and people infected with Hansen's disease. Don't feel guilty. Just share what you have.

Q. What do you think of the concept that my enemy is my lover?
A. It reminds me of what Mary Frances Clark, the founder of the B.V.M. community, used to say: "I have no fear as long as you are working unitedly." It also reminds me of a story. One day a woman infected with Hansen's disease came to our hospital for treatment. She had been there only a few days when I walked in and said, "I'm not going to be here for a week. North American surgeons are coming to operate on children with deformities and I'm going to interpret for them." This woman came up to me and said, "What are you talking about? What children? Where?" I told her the details and she said, "I have a grandson who was born with multiple birth defects—webbed hands, cleft palate, and pigeon-toed feet. He can't go to school because he can't walk or write.

Could you please help him?" I said, "Call your family and tell them to bring him on Sunday when they are going to review the children. I'll make sure he gets checked first."

Out of the hundreds of children, the boy was chosen for surgery. The grandmother stayed overnight with him at the hospital and said to me the next day, "I remembered a promise I made to God when my grandson was born. I said I would do anything to help him. Last night I realized God answered my prayer by using Hansen's disease to get him help. When I first got the disease, I used to cry, 'Why me?' Now, I realize it was a blessing in disguise." Talk about an enemy as a lover! Since then, this boy has had several successful surgeries and can smile, walk, write, and attend school. The medical team even gives him two new pairs of orthopedic shoes a year. God works in mysterious ways.

SISTER ANNIE CREDIDIO

"Dear friends, let us love one another, because love is from God, and everyone who loves . . . knows God. There is no fear in love, but perfect love drives out fear."
                                    - 1 John 4:7, 4:19

"We are all children of the sun."
**Jorge Luis Delgado, Inca Shaman and Author
of *Andean Awakening***

Jorge Luis is a recognized teacher of Incan spirituality and an experienced mountain guide. He has been invited to the United States, Canada, Belgium, the Netherlands, and Turkey to lecture on Incan wisdom and culture and its meaning in our lives today. Jorge Luis is an indigenous Peruvian of Aymara heritage who has worked as a tour guide in the Sacred Valley and around Machu Picchu and Lake Titicaca for more than twenty years.

Jorge is a modern Inca chacaruna who effortlessly blends his life as a shaman with his duties as a business and family man. He has worked with notable people such as Bo Bingham (grandson of Machu Picchu explorer Hiram Bingham) and authors Don Miguel Ruiz (*The Four Agreements*) and David Childress (*The Lost Cities* series). He is also in personal contact with the Andean priests and indigenous people living in the Sacred Valley.

Jorge Luis Delgado is the founder of Kontiki Tour Company and has built several hotels in Cusco and on the shores of Lake Titicaca. His collection of antique textiles and artifacts is on display in his museum at Taypikala Hotel in Cusco.

Jorge has been interviewed by journalists in Europe and North America and was featured in the BBC television series *Everyman*. He also represents the Inca nation at international gatherings of elders such as Earth Works for Humanity. He speaks Spanish, English, and three indigenous languages and lives with his wife and three children in Puno, Peru.

JORGE LUIS DELGADO

Q. Can you tell me about your spiritual path?

A. When I was young, I didn't want to follow my traditional roots, even though my mother was a healer. So I tried to escape from metaphysical and shamanic things and became a businessman and scientific tour guide. At that time, I didn't have a picture of myself as a spiritual teacher. Now I'm still a businessman and tour guide, but I'm also a chacaruna, an Inca shaman who uses stones and feathers to heal. It's a joy to share my Inca traditions and experiences with others. Of course, I love and respect everyone's path—their own possibilities and light.

I used to work as a guide for Don Miguel Ruiz when he took his groups to Peru. He would teach the Toltec ways and I would teach the Inca. We always commented on how similar everything was. When he had a heart attack, I went to visit him in Las Vegas. I went to Las Vegas for spiritual reasons (laughing)! I asked him, "What happened during your heart attack? Where did you go?" He replied, "I went with the masters. I saw that they are all working to bring spirituality back to everyone on the planet."

This confirmed all our legends and prophesies about returning to the cycle of light. Sometimes we think the light is just for good people. Who is to say who is good? The light is for everyone. Everyone has an inner sun. It's great to see that and know that this transformation is happening. Our ego sometimes says, "I would like to see it all, the whole transformation." But we must remember that our brothers and sisters who built Machu Picchu didn't expect to see it finished. They just put their love, service, and wisdom into each stone. Today we can still feel it. It's one of the Seven Wonders of the World. It expresses the *apukunas* (mountain spirits), *Pachamama* (Mother Earth), and mountains in an extraordinary way.

INCA SHAMAN

Q. Can you tell me more about this cycle of light and the prophecies?

A. Two years ago, we held a gathering of native elders from all over the world—Apaches, Hopi, Navahos, and many other nations. This gathering was about reconnecting with each other and Mother Earth. It was about fulfilling the prophecy of the eagle (North American native peoples) and the condor (South American native peoples) flying together. So the elders' presence in South America and my presence in the U.S. show that this prophecy is manifesting.

This prophecy has to do with *munay*, *llancay*, and *yachay*— our inner sun. It's the endless spring of love, service, and wisdom from which we all come. We can make our lives extraordinary by putting love, service, and wisdom in everything we do. When we use only our mind, we sometimes see life as ordinary. And everything we do becomes a little hard. Work can seem like a punishment. But when we put our love, service, and wisdom into what we do, it becomes joyful. We open our creativity and connect to the Mother. This expands our consciousness into abundance and prosperity. The new cycle we are entering is called *pachakuti* or *taripay pacha* in Quechua, an indigenous Peruvian language. It means, "Return to the Essence of the Cosmos," and is about finding yourself and your inner sun. In the Inca tradition, we are all children of the sun. And we expectantly await the transition back from night (the last five hundred-year cycle) to day (this five hundred-year cycle). During this transition, we become a bridge from the Father Sun (*Tayta Inti*) to the Mother Earth (*Pachamama*), and from the Mother Earth to the Father Sun. Our lives become the message of the inner sun.

So what is your message? The message you give others depends on the message you give yourself. Is the message you give yourself about love, service, and wisdom? Or is it about judging and punishing yourself, weighing yourself down with heavy energies of the past? Be aware of how you talk to yourself. This will help you see where you are in your relationships. Sometimes the mind will try to trick you and say, *You're already spiritually connected. You pray, meditate, and even levitate!* But with your heart, with your inner sun, you must always ask, "How is my relationship to Mother Earth . . . to Father Sun . . . to my family . . . to my neighbors . . . to my past? How am I practicing my love, service, and wisdom in these areas?"

We experienced things during the night, the cycle of darkness, which we thought were true—that our parents told us were true. And now, with the return to the light, we see that the truth is the light. And it's important to see from which spring we drink. Do we drink from love or fear? The disease of fear brings about separation. When we separate, we can't feel oneness. I notice this even among spiritual people who say, "I belong to this group so I can't believe in other traditions." It's the mind that says this and creates this separation.

There is a beautiful Andean legend that says we are here to expand what we are. But what is that? It is *munay, llancay,* and *yachay. Munay* is the Law of Love (First Inca Law). How do we know about love? From our parents or spouses? Sometimes these are only thoughts. We know love only when we experience it. The most joyful moments in our lives are when we feel love. It's something we can't measure. And our minds want to because they are rational—and rational comes from "ratio," meaning "to measure." So if we can't measure love, how do we know we are expanding it?

The mind will say, *You already know about love. You've got a certificate, the initiation to be a master.* This is because the mind always wants proof that you've succeeded. But the legend does not say that. It simply asks us to practice love. And the best way to practice is through sharing it. This practice helps you feel when you are coming from love versus when you are coming from fear. Because sometimes we share fear in the name of love! It may be something we learned from our parents.

So start by loving yourself. Take a moment each day to enjoy yourself. You will become more aware of who you are and how it feels to love. Then you can share it. The legend says that as you start to love yourself, you can expand this love like an endless stream—to the Mother, the Father, your family, your neighbors, and your past.

The word *ñahui* in Aymara and Quechua (indigenous languages) means "eye." It also means "past." So how do you see your past? If you don't love your experiences, then you must release them. You don't have to carry these heavy energies. When you let them go, you let your life flow. You become a portal to the Father Sun, expressing who you are in your love, service, and wisdom. It isn't about a specific moment at a special event. It is about practicing love in your relationships every day. Every day you have the opportunity to grow your love, service, and wisdom.

But the mind always asks, *How can I get to a higher consciousness of love?* which is called *tucuy munayniyoc.* You are born with your highest level of consciousness. As you practice love, the cosmos sends a messenger in the form of a hummingbird that flies above your head to gather your nectar. That's the image of the legend—that as you open your petals, you become a beautiful flower sharing nectar from your heart, your inner sun.

We are all children of the sun. And our inner sun is the child within that was never wounded. So whatever we experience, that part remains unscathed. But when we come into this reality, we encounter some heavy energies. The Mother Earth is always ready to help us transform them. Crystals and precious stones are part of this process. We are not children of casualty. We are children of love who have the same attributes as the Father Sun and Mother Earth. And in this new day, we are awakening. Some had flashlights and awoke before the sunrise. Others are arising at its first rays. Still others will need a strong cup of coffee to get there. Whatever the pace, everyone will awaken in this cycle.

In the Inca tradition, we believe in one thousand-year cycles—five hundred years of day and five hundred years of night. We believe we are in the tenth cycle or *pachakuti*, which is five thousand years. Many other traditions, like those in Mexico, also believe in these cycles. For example, Don Miguel Ruiz was saying that the sixth age started in 1992. For us, the new *pachakuti* also began in 1992, with the full sun coming in 2012. As the sun rises, we become aware of our essence. We are the children of the Father Sun and Mother Earth. We are *munay*, *llancay*, and *yachay*. We don't need any special training or certificate to be who we are. We just have to release the heavy energies that don't come from love—that create resistance to sharing our gifts.

Q. In the U.S. we say, "Do what you love and the money will follow." However, some are afraid to take this risk. Even those who do often don't experience abundance. Why?

A. It's because of fear. Fear is a disease. In the movie *Apocalypto*, there is a scene in which some frightened natives are running away from something when they encounter a joyous tribe. They ask the tribal elder for permission to pass through his land. He agrees. Then the tribal elder's son says something like, "What was that?" The elder replies, "Fear. Don't let it seep into you." We believe that fear is part of our lives. That it is normal. So, from where does this belief come? Our mind—and the things that trained our mind— our family, society, and history. During the cycle of night, we believed what the mind said, that we would be happy if we achieved a certain level of success or social status. Yes, being successful is good. But only if it brings more joy.

INCA SHAMAN

A student showed me the movie *The Secret* when I was teaching at the Omega Institute. He asked me, "What do you think of it?" I replied, "I think it's great. It teaches people how to manifest things in magical ways. The student said, "What else do you think?" I said, "You can manifest anything you want—a million dollars, a nice house, or car. But it doesn't guarantee you joy. True joy comes from being with yourself and your inner sun. It comes from releasing the heavy energies that hold you in fear. This fear comes not only from us, but also from past generations. And with the new sunrise, we have the opportunity to release it and become the first rays of light. We can give our fear to the Mother and she can transform it. Our light is shifting the planet. As we change our way of being, we also change the Earth—because we are one with the Mother. Our healing is her healing. As the Earth and we become healthier, all the fragrances and manifestations of life become more beautiful and joyous.

We sometimes worry about our economy and environment. We often think the problem is political and that we need the right plan—we need to choose between capitalism and socialism. But these are just thoughts about ways of organizing things. The truth is that any approach will work if we have consciousness. That is the solution to everything. A civilization with consciousness wouldn't permit starvation or pollution because our sense of oneness wouldn't allow it. And this sense of oneness comes from each of us finding our inner sun. So what allows these problems? Fear. It weakens our human immune system, leaving us vulnerable to separation and conflict.

In the days before the last night (the last five hundred-year cycle), we used to have universities like Machu Picchu, Sillustani, and Tiahuanaco. Now, when people visit these sites, they often ask me what the buildings were used for. They think every structure had a specific purpose because that's how we build today. We have houses where people live, churches

JORGE LUIS DELGADO

where people worship, hospitals where people heal, and so on. But in the Incan societies, everything was multidimensional. The Incas believed that the Father Sun, Mother Earth, Milky Way, and all the elements and natural kingdoms were dancing together. They had that sort of awareness of life. So sites like Machu Picchu were about finding our place in the universe. They are cities of the universe—the true universities. They are about finding your heart, your spirit, and your inner sun. They are places where you become aware of who you really are. Nowadays, our universities do a good job with the mind, but they neglect everything else that we are. The medicine for the new day is our inner sun. It is the light and spirit of our true essence.

So your question is not just about abundance. It's about awareness of this abundance. When we see it as multidimensional, we open to our creativity and unique gifts. One on side, we have *munay*, the Law of Love. And on the other, we have *llancay*, the Law of Work (Second Inca Law). Some dictionaries define work as a kind of toil or punishment. In Spanish, the word work is *trabajo*. *Traba* means "obstacle" and *abajo* means "down." The literal translation is "an obstacle that brings us down!" But *llancay* is about service. It is the opportunity to give to Mother Earth, to bring abundance and prosperity to everyone. We all have this consciousness, called *tucuy llancayniyoc*. And with it, we can manifest whatever we want. But when we reach this level, all we want to manifest is more joy and life. *Yachay*, the Law of Wisdom (Third Inca Law), is the other state of consciousness. At the higher levels of wisdom, called *sonccoqui*, everything in life becomes joyous and abundant. Our fear melts away and we see infinite possibility.

Every one of us—business leaders, healers, and teachers—have the opportunity to be of service by creating work and abundance. In this time of *pachakuti*, we are returning to the essence of the cosmos. To return, we need to repeat how the cosmos came into being. First, there was chaos. Then beauty, peace, and harmony. So right now, we are in chaos and everything is turned upside down. Some people are experiencing this in a severe way. It all depends on where you are. If you are in your inner sun, nothing will perturb you. You will fly and flow with life. But if you are in your mind or ego, you will struggle. These experiences are not easy but they will help many.

We must remember that every cycle brings changes to the planet. When we look back at our history, we see there have been many changes. Some people feel guilty about the changes we have caused Mother Earth. Instead of feeling guilty, we should love the Mother and ourselves and do the best we can. When we love the Mother, she reciprocates. Everything we do should be in *ayni*, or reciprocity—not only when dealing with people, but also with every facet of life. The return of the children of the sun is not about one Inca ruling the cosmos. It's about the return of consciousness. It's similar to what some believe about the return of Jesus and Christ consciousness. In the Inca tradition, everyone has an inner sun. Everyone is returning to their essence. So we are becoming active. We are gathering to pray, dance, and do ceremonies with the Father Sun and the Mother Earth.

As we children of the sun become aware, we bring this awareness to the Mother. When I say Mother, I mean all of us, including Mother Earth. Everybody brings a unique gift. Who you are is your message and this message is important. Watch your mind like a puma, the animal that represents our life on Earth. (The condor represents the heavens and the snake the underworld.) See what your expression to the cosmos is every day. Are you acting from limitation and struggle, or abundance and joy? Each morning, start the day by remembering your essence, instead of all the things you have

JORGE LUIS DELGADO

to do. In the Inca tradition, we look to the East and connect our inner sun with the Father Sun. Then we greet all the cells in our body, all our little suns. We greet them to heal ourselves. In Spanish, the word greet is *saludar*, which means "to give health." We greet everybody else, so why not greet ourselves? This practice helps you love yourself. The more you love yourself, the more you can expand it to others.

People used to tell me that it was hard to love themselves. But I would reply, "I know you can. You want to know why? If you can hate yourself, you can love yourself. The emotion of hate is just the flip side." Their faces would change immediately and they would say, "You're right!" I'd go on to say that it's actually easier to love yourself. You can learn this by using something you already know. When you see a loved one that you haven't seen in a while, you open your arms wide and forget everything except the joy you feel. That joy comes from your inner sun, your spirit, which is always happy and at peace. Give this same joy to yourself every day. Practice by shining your inner sun with that of the Father Sun and the Divine Central Sun (the father of the father sun). You will see that your whole body is light, that you are just an apparition who is always changing depending on how you feel and flow.

We are light. That is what we are. So open our arms and bring your right hand to your heart with love. Feeling this love allows you to share it in reciprocity or *ayni* with everything and everyone. Now bring your left hand to your solar plexus without fear. If you feel fear, take your left hand from your solar plexus and give the fear to the Mother. This practice helps you remember who you are and expands you in love, service, and wisdom. When you put who you are into what you do, your life becomes extraordinary.

And what is the difference between extraordinary and ordinary? It is just extra (joke intended). And what is that extra?

It's your spirit, your inner sun, the essence of who you are. You are the most precious ray of the sun. You are the most precious expression of the Earth. You don't have to go any-where to get a certificate. You just have to be present with who you are and share your gifts.

Q. What do you think of the concept that my enemy is my lover?

A. It's an interesting way to grab your attention if you are clear that the enemy is yourself. Whatever you see outside is just a reflection of you. This way of looking allows you to see if you are really with yourself, or if you are only with what you believe about yourself. What we believe has to do with our history. And we project this history onto others all the time. Then, as we mature, we start to become interested in spiri-tuality. And we discover, "Oh, it wasn't about them. It was about me (laughing)!"

JORGE LUIS DELGADO

"An authentically empowered person lives in love. Love is not a passive state. It is an active force. It is the force of the soul. There is nothing that cannot be healed by love. There is nothing but love."

- Gary Zukav

"Who is wise? He who learns from all people."
Rabbi Bruce Dollin, Senior Rabbi,
Hebrew Educational Alliance

Rabbi Bruce Dollin has served as the Hebrew Educational Alliance's rabbi since August, 1994. Before moving to Denver, he served as the spiritual leader of Adath Shalom in Dover, New Jersey for eight years. Rabbi Dollin received rabbinical ordination from the Jewish Theological Seminary in 1986, receiving a master's degree in Judaica at the same time. He spent a year in Israel studying at Hebrew University in Jerusalem from 1982 to 1983. The rabbi holds a bachelor's degree in Judaic literature from the University of Judaism, and completed his undergraduate studies in psychology at the University of Santa Clara. Rabbi Dollin is an active member of the Rocky Mountain Rabbinical Council and serves on the boards of the Central Agency for Jewish Education and the Jewish Community Center. He and his wife, Tammy Dollin, have four children, Yonaton, Yeshai, Akiva, and Aviva.

Q. What experiences put you on your spiritual path?

A. I loved being Jewish, especially as a young person growing up in Albuquerque, New Mexico and participating in Jewish youth groups. My Jewish life felt special, warm, and important. I wanted to explore it more fully and rabbinical school offered a way to do that. Interestingly, I attended a Jesuit university where I interacted with several of my Jesuit professors. I admired their education and commitment to religious faith. I wanted to find the same as a Jew. After college, I went straight to rabbinical school.

Q. How did these experiences change you?

A. My experience in rabbinical school changed me significantly. I saw very serious, smart people dedicating their lives to Jewish learning and holding it up as an ideal. I always had taken my studies seriously but this was a whole new level. I loved every minute of rabbinical school and decided to spend my life as an observant Jew, teaching Judaism to others. Learning and teaching are my ways to serve God.

Q. What changes are you noticing about your life and the world?

A. My path now involves leading a 1,000 family congregation. This responsibility is a far cry from rabbinical school, where all I had to do was study. Now I must make Judaism relevant to people, some of whom have little Jewish education and experience living as a Jew. At the same time, I must lead a large staff of Jewish professionals, interact with the board of directors, and oversee the many programs of the congregation. It has been a major challenge balancing the organization's needs with staying true to my central mission: bringing people into Jewish communal life.

Q. What changes are others noticing about you?

A. As a young man, I believed people were basically good and that evil was caused by confused individuals who could be changed with attention and good will. I do not believe this anymore. Since 9/11, I see most people as good but some are clearly evil, capable of killing the innocent for their own twisted reasons. Now I am a bit more skeptical of people's intentions, but also more forgiving of bad behavior, as I come to understand that living in this world is a great challenge for everyone.

Q. What has been the most challenging part of your path?

A. I have been a pulpit rabbi for twenty-two years. When I first entered the rabbinate, I was filled with ideas on how to mold people into my image of a committed and observant Jew. I suspect people see me now as calmer and more patient. It is hard for people to change, and when they genuinely do, they do so very slowly. I have come to accept that I may never know if I have helped someone change for the better. That is where I rely on my faith in Jewish life. The more people connect to religious life, the better human beings they become.

Q. What is your earliest memory? Why do you remember it?

A. My earliest memory is sitting with my mother on the couch and her telling me that I would begin preschool the next day. I was terrified and did not like my first couple of preschools. This was a time of profound change as I began learning from teachers outside my home. Of all the people I respect, the vast majority are teachers.

Q. Who are your mentors? What have you learned from them?

A. My mentors have always been teachers. In high school and college, my humanities teachers had the biggest impact. They introduced me to exploring the meaning of life, channeling my enthusiasm into questions such as, "Why do we exist on this earth?" In rabbinical school, the teachers were all excellent, so my mentors became those who cared most about their students' emotional, spiritual, and intellectual development. Since entering the pulpit rabbinate, I look to mentors who are kind and attentive to congregants' personal needs. As Rabbi Abraham Joshua Heschel once said, "When I was younger, I admired smart men. Now that I am older, I admire kind men."

Q. What is the greatest challenge facing society?

A. I see three major challenges. The first is religious extremism. I fear people who see their view of God and the world as correct and all others interpretations as wrong. Piety begins with humility, which helps us see that we have only a partial understanding of the truth. I cannot grasp how someone can justify killing in God's name.

The other challenges are narcissism and materialism. Our sacred texts instruct, "If I am not for myself, who will be for me? If I am only for myself, what am I?" We do not have problems "being for ourselves." We *do* face significant prob-

RABBI BRUCE DOLLIN

lems being "only for ourselves." We place too much emphasis on wealth and not enough on giving. Meaning in life relates to how much we give—in our friendships, marriages, and parental roles. I once met a philanthropist who said that if he could, he would give away everything and die penniless. Our society needs more people like that.

9. What advice would you give someone just starting his or her spiritual path?

Q. Be patient. It takes a lifetime. I sometimes am asked why we read the Torah, the Old Testament's first five books, every year, year after year. My answer is that with each reading, we learn something new. This is because we have changed. Our understanding of God, revelation, ritual, and good and evil develops over decades.

Q. What are your practices for connecting to your higher purpose?

A. I read everything I can. I learn much about my purpose from reading how others understand the world. Judaism is filled with ritual that brings the community together. I connect to my higher purpose by throwing my lot in with the community and the people of Israel.

Q. How do you use these practices when you get out of balance?

A. I try not to get out of balance. At our synagogue, we have a mission to provide our community with opportunities for learning, praying, and performing acts of kindness. We measure everything we do against this mission. Our mission keeps us in balance as a synagogue and keeps me in balance as a rabbi and Jewish man.

Q. How do you balance planning with remaining open to opportunity?

A. I come back to our mission. It is organized yet flexible enough to take advantage of unexpected opportunity. Speakers, teachers, new curricula, and staff brainstorming keep our synagogue program fresh, while giving us the chance to grow the program and ourselves as Jews.

Q. If you received $100,000, how would you spend it?

A .Unfortunately, $100,000 does not buy much these days. But, if you were to give it to me, I would invest it in our excellent staff. Our synagogue is about the people who work here and their interaction, as Jewish professionals, with our synagogue community.

Q. If you had thirty seconds with someone in an elevator, what three things would you tell the person to do to be joyful, peaceful, and whole?

A. The answer will be different for each of us. My sense of wholeness comes from reading and thinking and bringing what I learn to others. I am careful to balance my marriage, family, and work. There is no peace, joy, and wholeness if I neglect the people I love most. Be humble and learn from everything in life. Give generously of yourself and your money to those who need it.

Q. What books or resources have helped you the most? Why?

A. My favorite texts are the Book of Proverbs and a Talmudic text called, Chapters of the Fathers (*Pirkei Avot*). These texts tell us how to live a meaningful and moral life. I base my rabbinate and life as an adult Jew on the wisdom found in these texts.

Q. What would you like to be written on your tombstone?

A. I would like the following quote from Chapters of the Fathers: "Who is wise? He who learns from all people."

RABBI BRUCE DOLLIN

"What you are will show in what you do."
                                    - Thomas Edison

9

"Persevere because the Lord is there."
Charlie Duke, Apollo 16 Astronaut and Moon Walker
Cofounder of Duke Ministry for Christ

Charlie Duke was born in Charlotte, NC in 1935. Led by a desire to serve his country, Duke attended the U.S. Naval Academy in Annapolis, Maryland. Following graduation, he was commissioned into the U.S. Air Force, and thus began a life-long love of flying. Over the years as a fighter pilot, test pilot, and then encouraged by his commandant Chuck Yeager to become an Apollo astronaut, this love of adventure grew to the pinnacle of achievement when on April 20, 1972, he, along with John Young, landed on the surface of the moon. Their stay on the moon was a record-setting seventy-one hours and fourteen minutes. During Apollo's three-day return from the moon, Duke experienced a space walk with the third crewmember, Ken Mattingly.

Apollo 16 returned home to a heroes' welcome, with Duke, Young, and Mattingly each receiving the NASA Distinguished Service Medal. Since Duke's retirement from NASA in 1975, he has been very active in business. Duke also served in the Air Force Reserves as Special Assistant to the Commander of USAF Recruiting Service, meeting all goals of recruitment of engineers and doctors. He traveled extensively speaking at schools and universities as part of Project Warrior. The National Aeronautics and Space Administration appointed him to the NASA Advisory Council. He is currently the owner of Charlie Duke Enterprises, which has produced one book, *Moonwalker* (co-authored with his wife), and two videos, *Moonwalker* and *Walk on the Moon, Walk with the Son*. He is also president of Duke Investments and, with his wife Dotty, cofounded Duke Ministry for Christ.

CHARLIE DUKE

Q. What experiences put you on your spiritual path?

A. First, was the obvious change I saw in my wife, Dotty, when she came to the Lord in October 1975. I watched her change from sadness to joy. Over the next two and a half years, she became the most loving wife even though I hadn't changed. That was very significant. Second, I had grown up in church and had always known about Jesus but it wasn't a personal relationship. It was more of a Sunday relationship based on head knowledge. Yes, Jesus is Lord but he is out there somewhere and I am basically in charge of my life. That changed in April 1978 after a weekend Bible study. There, I came to the realization that Jesus is either the Son of God or he is a liar. After studying the scriptures from Genesis to Revelation, it was obvious to me that Jesus is the Savior. I was sitting in my automobile and said, "Lord, I give you my life." Then, a peace came over me and I knew it was real. Jesus had come from my head to my heart. After that, I had an insatiable desire to read the Bible and grow in the Lord. It's been going for thirty years now.

Q. How did these experiences change you?

A. Scriptures are what I call the Manufacturer's handbook for life. If we apply the principles of scripture, we reflect the character of God in every area of our lives. I began to see that the Lord wanted me to love my wife the way he loves the church—which is one hundred percent. So, I applied these principles to my marriage, family, business, and so on. and everything got better. Now that I have internalized these principles, I am filled with love for my wife and family and am more at peace. I used to have an explosive temper and now it's gone. "The old is gone and the new is come," as the scripture says. (2 Corinthians 5:17)

Q. What changes are you noticing about your life?

A. Scripture says, "Don't exasperate your children (Ephesians 6:4, Colossians 3:21)." As a father, there were times I expected too much from them—especially when they were very young. It's hard to get a five-year-old to respond to military discipline and I was that kind of dad because I was trained in the armed forces. I had a critical spirit toward them and was speaking words of criticism. Then, I started reading Proverbs and James about the power of the tongue. (James 3:8-3:11, Proverbs 15:4, 18:21) I learned that words have power. God spoke the world into existence. So, my words can speak life or death to my children. Words of death are curses such as "You are stupid son. You will never learn."

As husbands, fathers, and heads of the household our words have great power. The Lord showed me this and I repented and asked my boys for forgiveness. Then, I began speaking blessings into their lives while still disciplining in the way that the Lord instructs. Our relationships began to heal. Now, the boys are grown and we have nine wonderful grandchildren. We don't always see eye-to-eye on every subject but we enjoy our family reunions and spend a lot of time together. It's a terrific relationship and I am trying to be a good godly example to my sons and grandchildren. To sum up, watch the power of the tongue and be careful what you speak.

Q. What changes are others noticing about you?
A. Dotty's and my marriage is just so strong now. We put Jesus first in our relationship, first in our lives. And Jesus was able to change us on the inside. He has done that and continues to do so. We both realize how much we have changed.

Q. What has been the most challenging part of your path?
A. The biggest challenge was my relationship with my wife. Our marriage was pretty far-gone when she came to the Lord. We were verging on divorce. To start loving her, as the Lord wanted me to, would have been impossible without the Holy Spirit. But the Lord has healed our relationship and we are very content and happy now.

Q. What is your earliest memory? Why do you remember it?

CHARLIE DUKE

A. The first memory I have is when we lived in Columbia, South Carolina. I was riding my tricycle down the sidewalk with my twin brother and our nurse was following us. Down the street from our house, the city was cutting down this enormous pine tree. We watched it come crashing down. I was four years old and it was the biggest crash—the biggest event—I had ever seen.

Q. Who are your mentors? What have you learned from them?

A. In the early days, the Lord sent people to our house. One of the first was a Romanian named Ilie Coroama. He was very influential in our early walk with the Lord. He taught us about the power of God and hearing the voice of God. Every couple of months, he would come to our home and spend a couple of days. We also would travel to Romania and Western Europe with him. In addition, there was a Ukrainian man named Ausiclus Ziedermanus—whom the Lord sent to help us grow in the Spirit—and leaders of the Full Gospel Businessmen's Fellowship. Though I don't know them personally, two people I respect and admire are Dr. James Dobson and William R. "Bill" Bright who is now deceased.

Q. What is the greatest challenge facing society?

A. As far as world peace, it is probably militant Islam. On the other hand, there seems to be a falling away from the authority of scripture in the Christian church, at least in this country. I don't see that so much in Africa, the Middle East, or Central and South America where the church is growing. We seem to have it so good in America that we have become a post-Christian, "Who needs God now?" kind of society.

Q. Follow-up question: What are the consequences of this attitude?

A. You see it in the moral fiber of our nation, in the laws being passed that stand against godly principles. You see it in the overall moral decay with regards to corruption, sexual scandal, and the decline in values such as respect, character, and integrity. There is just a looseness now that wasn't around when I was a kid.

Q. What advice would you give someone just starting his or her spiritual path?

A. It's important to teach perseverance, to say, "Hang in there," because there are going to be some discouraging moments. For example, in my walk, it's two steps forward, one step back. When you get buffeted by life's trials and tribulations, don't get discouraged. Ground yourself in The Word of God through daily Bible reading and prayer. I'm not so much a Bible studier in my private time. I just read and allow the Lord to speak to me through scripture. From that, I have learned perseverance. That's one of the most important characteristics we Christians can have. Persevere because the Lord is there.

Q. What are your practices for connecting to your higher purpose?

A. Reading the scripture and allowing the Lord to speak to me. Praying—doing devotionals—in the morning and night. Listening to God's direction for my life.

Q. How do you use these practices when you get out of balance?

A. We're human. When I start to get angry, it is not of an explosive nature. That's not there anymore. But, if I raise my voice to my wife, the Lord instantly convicts me and I confess. Scripture says, "When we sin, if we confess our sins, he is faithful and just and will forgive and cleanse us." (1 John 1:9) When I confess and ask the offended party for forgiveness, then a peace returns to our relationship.

Q. How do you balance planning with remaining open to opportunity?

A. I am open to change in my daily schedule, partially because I am retired and don't have to go to an office. I do write out

CHARLIE DUKE

my schedule regarding projects that the Lord brings and wants me to get done. We receive a lot of requests over the Internet. Sometimes, one will catch my eye. Right now, there are some kids who sent a questionnaire for a program they would like to do that's similar to Walter Cronkite's old show *You Are There*. In that show, Cronkite reenacted historical events using a news report format. I generally don't respond to that stuff because I get hundreds of requests but this one sticks out in my mind.

Q. If you received $100,000, how would you spend it?

A. We have a Duke Ministry for Christ that is a nonprofit corporation. We would put it into that to support ministries around the world. We don't earn a living from our ministry. We don't even take salaries, only the occasional travel expense. So, when people send us a dollar, the dollar goes straight into the ministry. Through the ministry, the Lord leads us to Africa, India, and Romania. If people there can't afford to pay us, we pay our own way.

We also support Ilie Coroama's *Walk in the Light* Ministries— his orphanage and home for unwed mothers in Romania— and the Jesus Film Project, which is a powerful ministry of the Campus Crusade for Christ. We have a lot of other indigenous ministries in Third World countries—two in India, one in Iran, and so on. So, when we receive money, we pray saying, "Lord, where would you have us use this?" Then, we do as he directs.

Q. If you had thirty seconds with someone in an elevator, what three things would you tell him or her to do to be joyful, peaceful, and whole?

A. I usually carry a small pamphlet of *Walk on the Moon, Walk with the Son*. I would say to him or her, "If you need support, let me give you something that tells about what the Lord has done in my life. Then I'd say, "Have a good day and God bless you."

Q. What books or resources have helped you the most? Why?

A. For me, the primary resource is the scripture. My wife and I pray together in the mornings and evenings, reading short devotionals such as Good News from our church and Daily Bread. In my private time, scripture frequently speaks to me about direction. I have not had time lately to read Christian books but early on in our walk with the Lord, He brought us many encouraging books. They were more about testimony rather than systematic study. Ilie Coroama's book *Walk in the Light* in an amazing read about his miraculous escape from Romania. I have read a lot of books about healing, deliverance, and walking in The Spirit and hearing The Voice of God. All of them were helpful. Now, we have a whole library full of them.

Q. Please share the story you told about your dad in *Walk on the Moon, Walk with the Son.*

A. Several years ago, I had a discussion with my dad in which I told him that the Lord loved him, could heal him, and give him peace. To build his faith, I shared a story about our friends who pray to the Lord every time they get on an airplane. They ask that he surround the plane with angels to carry them safely to their destination. In one of those flights, God opened my friends' eyes and they saw an angel sitting on the wing of the airplane. My dad chuckled and said, "If I ever see an angel, he had better have on a parachute!" I replied, "Dad, I pray you see an angel."

That memory had faded when, many years later, I was in California and my wife called. She said, "You're mom wants you to come home quickly. Your dad is not expected to live much longer." My friend Ilie Coroama took me to the airport so I could get on the next flight to South Carolina. Ilie is very faithful in prayer. God has given him a number of dreams and visions. So I asked him to pray as I got on the plane home. I arrived shortly after my dad died. As my family and I were

CHARLIE DUKE

gathering and comforting each other, the phone rang. It was my wife. She said, "Call Ilie, he has a word from the Lord for you." So I called Ilie and he said, "I was praying for your dad at two o'clock this afternoon and the Lord gave me a vision. He showed me two angels coming to gather your dad and that he would die very soon. I said, "Praise the Lord, my dad was dying while you were praying." (Two o'clock California time is five o'clock South Carolina time, the hour my dad passed.) Then Ilie said, "Charlie, I have seen angels before but I have never seen angels wearing parachutes. Why would angels do that?" I replied, "I don't know. Let's pray about it." Two weeks later, the Lord brought to mind that conversation I had had with my dad about his wanting any angel he saw to have on a parachute.

This beautiful story really built my faith. God knows every detail about us—every thought, every action. The scripture talks about the hairs on our heads being numbered. And that not one sparrow falls to the ground unless the Lord knows about it. (Matthew 10:29-30) The power, immensity, and love of God revealed in that story so reinforces what the Bible says. And, it also shows that God has a sense of humor. To my dad, he was saying, "Okay, I will show you angels with parachutes!"

10

"You are no mistake."
Jeffrey Duvall, Cofounder
Men's Council Project and Men's Leadership Alliance

Jeffrey is cofounder of the Men's Council Project and the Men's Leadership Alliance, which offer men heart and soul inspired courses, including the Art of Leadership training program. For over twenty years, he has guided men's healing and inspiration retreats around the country as an inquiry into the blessings of manhood. The work is centered on connection to personal mythology and empowerment through the individual's life story and soul voice. Jeffrey offers one-on-one personal mentoring and council support for adults and adolescents. Jeffrey is the author of the well received book, *Stories of Men, Meaning, and Prayer*, written in conjunction with James Churches. He is a wilderness rites of passage guide for youth and adults and assists individuals and groups in creating community rituals and blessing ways. He is also a Four Gateways Coach© based on the healing studies of Dr. Thomas Daly, world elder, teacher, and visionary. He lives with his wife and son in Colorado.

Q. Please share a bit about your book and what you do?

A. My book *Stories of Men, Meaning, and Prayer* was an attempt to share reflections of modern man with the public, as well as our ancient experience. Even though the book is about my experiences with men, it's not gender exclusive. Over the past twenty-five years, I have seen that when men gather, we're not separate from the rest of humanity. We putting aside gender interactive living for a while to find out who we really are. It is a moment in time of focusing, shedding old skin, and helping each other get along to become better world citizens. There is a power, beauty, and humility in this process as we further our compassion and develop a kind, fierce presence. What I'm doing with men is equally, if

JEFFREY DUVALL

not more, for the Earth.

As time goes on, I feel I know less and less about how the mind wants to define things. So many of our beliefs are no longer useful or inclusive enough. One of my elders said, "Your beliefs will imprison you." Yet we must have them and continually soften them so we can leave our blessing, our service. In some way, we're part of a continuum with no hierarchy. We're each individually important. That's how I work with people. Keeping this continuum of ancient experience alive and fresh in the new day.

Q. What experiences put you on your spiritual path?

A. I grew up in a blue-collar community in the 1950s and 1960s, where religion played a strong role. I was always in trouble and everything around me felt aggressive—my family, my religion, my culture, and myself. I had this that sense there must be more. I found more with my great grandparents and grandparents. Even though they were simple farmers, their homes were welcome places, which seemed to reflect what "more" was. When I sustained a major football injury in college, I was humbled and started to listen. I lived near Lake Superior and used to go there every day, being drawn to it without knowing why. The lake was a softening force whose presence started to change my wandering and elders began appearing into my life: an archbishop, an older woman who taught transcendental meditation, an old man who used to box for Al Capone and taught me how to chop wood and hold a tool (weapon), and another elder who showed me how to find wild mushrooms and see wild birds.

It's really the same story experienced by everybody who makes it. A lot of my friends didn't. They died of excess—

> "People say I am ripping off Native Americans. I reply that I am native, native of everything."

alcohol, fast cars, and AIDS. We would go way out on jour-

neys, trying to find some kind of spirit or freedom in a culture based on materialism.
Vietnam was happening and many of us realized that what we had grown up with wasn't the whole truth about our country. It did not work well for us, especially since our friends were getting killed in the war.

> "I knew I had to know my way among men to know my way in the world."

Around age thirty, I met a young woman who was a Buddhist and a cleaning lady. I told her, "I think I may end my life. Everything is based on some kind of career and I'm not interested in that. So I may never see you again." She replied, "Before you go, come see me." She was so kind that I had to honor her request. It's funny how kindness bestows that sort of power. So, I went to her and said, "I think I'm done. I'll be gone in a week." She replied, "There's a man in town I would like you to meet before you go." Again, I honored her request and went to the house of a psychologist where people were gathered around a Buddhist monk exiled from Tibet.

When I walked through the door, the monk who had been sleeping in the corner looked up at me and smiled. I don't know if I have ever let myself receive a smile like that before. He seemed to be saying, "Whoever you are, whatever you have done, you are welcome here." I sat, listened to stories, and had a cup of soup. Before I left, I asked the psychologist if he would be willing to talk with me. Out of kindness, he decided to see me whether I could pay or not. He helped me wake up and realize there are other ways that people are living. Nine months later, I found myself in Colorado studying the healing arts.

Q. How did these experiences change you?
A. For many of us, it takes a lot of reminders. So these people and experiences were mine. I don't believe in coincidences

JEFFREY DUVALL

and I gain solace from watching things unfold that are meant to. I continue to meet older people who are tracking similar matters—archetypes, spirit realms, and forces—that run through our bodies and live in us. These teachers show up in all different dimensions: sounds, images, nature, even a knothole in a tree. For example, I wrote in my book about a blind woman with whom I lived in the upper peninsula of Michigan for eleven days. We became friends as she took me through a process. I learned by getting into her way of doing things, her movements, and helping her with chores like picking up the mail and writing letters she dictated. The men, women, and youth I mentor also have become my teachers, even though it may have looked as though I was guiding.

> "There is great mystery and wonder running through every cell of your body. It is already who you are and is waiting for you to find it."

Over time, this spirit work has gotten simpler but not easier. I always have to check in asking, "Am I taking care of myself? Am I holding too much?" I have such a respect and humility for how ritual, prayer, and Spirit move through us. I am drawn to it like somebody who paints or writes every day. I'm fascinated with darkness, its absurdity, nastiness, and downright beauty. I want to know why it's showing up and what it wants from us.

These great abilities of the heart and soul don't necessarily come in just one lifetime. There's more of a generative fierceness. It's about not always needing to be nice and yet still saying, "Let's go the distance, let's work this out. Let's not give up on each other or our culture by creating more separation through blame." This is spiritual discipline. This is being in the fire together. Over the years, I have learned from lots of older people and they all have this fire. Being with them has given me, and anyone else who wants it, permission to pick up the torch. It's been a road of doing circles.

Q. What changes are you noticing about your life and the world?
A. Early in life, I saw aggression as a form of godliness or power. It's all I had so I got really good at it. However, even when I won, it never felt like victory. I kept wondering, *Is something missing or is this all there is?* Eventually, I realized we use aggression to find some divine aspect in ourselves that, ironically, is already there. After all these years, aggression is still the first tendency in many of us. But we have a say in how we respond and that becomes our work, especially as the aging process tempers our need to win.

I choose to soften, to be less aggressive and violent when presented with complexity—the fire of emotions, war, and righteousness. The word "righteousness" scares me. What I'm talking about goes beyond right and wrong, the words and boxes we create. It's about how I have changed from what I witnessed through my elders, the poets, and the thousands I have served. But, the question remains, "What do we do with the energy that is unleashed?" Do we manufacture what's been done time and time again? Or are we willing to take risks together? To do so, we need to acknowledge that the best and worst live in us, in me. I'll own it. All the things that scare people the most, like Hitler, are in me. When we move from this place of recognition, we have a chance to be different. Sometimes I wonder how much I have really changed. I'll miss something I was supposed to take care of and think, *How could I have done that?* Then there's relief. Maybe it's just a sign I need to stop and get a massage.

This project you have, there's an energy running through you. I love that energy in people. The old women in my life had that energy in the simplest ways. The men too, but if we are not careful, we can get tired and bitter. We put down the wood, stop stoking the fire, and let the pain of the world hurt

JEFFREY DUVALL

too much.

Q. What changes are others noticing about you?

A. I receive feedback all the time from people I have mentored and supported. Usually, they are grateful for my work. One of the elders who recently served at a retreat sent me a letter of appreciation asking if I was tired and wondering about a few comments I had made. During retreats, we also check in with each other in our circles, especially if energy lingers after something happens. All the feedback in the letters and check-ins is good. It's like a poem I can't resist even though it hurts a little. If I need to apologize to someone, I will. Or other times, I will say, "Maybe that's about something else going on in your life." I see myself as essentially the same as the retreat participants, no more or less.

For many years, people have questioned what I do. They ask, "Who do you think you are? What are your credentials?" They even say I am ripping off Native Americans. I reply that I am native, native of everything. Everything I use is in human culture. In the whole thing, there has been controversy. And that's okay. It's a creative process. I don't have to get it all right. After two decades, I have served a couple of generations—people I have known for a long time and their children who are now growing up. There's a sweet sadness in this because I see how beautiful it all is.

Q. What has been the most challenging part of your path?

A. Tracking my own evolution, aging, and passages. Knowing that I have failed in certain relationships, that I have not met the standards my ego places on me. Sometimes I get up and ask, "Do I really want to say yes today?" The elders say it's knowing our limits and still going beyond them, still experimenting with that frontier.

I see things differently than I did when I was a young man. I own my mistakes, if there really are such things, and question how I am spending my time. For example, how much time should I be away from my family? I don't take them for granted because I've seen others who walk the artistic path and I know I could lose it all. I could lose them. Beyond right and wrong, that's the way it happens sometimes. So, I need to decide how to parcel out my energies for my family and other interests. I also need to know when I am tired before I get exhausted and do something hurtful. All of us will do this anyway, no matter how much we try not to. I don't want to give my family up for some grand vision.

But I have this energy that runs through me and drives me. It feels very old, raw, dangerous, beautiful, creative, and re-generative. I love to see and feel this energy in people, including children. It is such a beautiful life force, such a beautiful archetype.

Q. What is your earliest memory? Why do you remember it?
A. Sometimes I think, *Did I really have a childhood? Or, did I have the one I think I did?* The answer is both yes and no. I don't have a lot of early memories because I grew up in an unhappy environment. There was a lot of love in my family but it often came out through the dark side.

I do have memories of experiencing severe migraines and not wanting to live. As a boy, I would go down to this wild river near my house and pass out from the migraines. It was a journey type thing after which I would wake up not knowing if I was alive or dead. Then I'd realize I was still alive. I also have memories of visiting my great aunt's and uncle's farm when I was between five and twelve years old. When we would pull up; my aunt would stop whatever she was doing and greet us. She would gather me up in her arms, all wrinkled and sun browned. This memory is something that stays alive in me.

Q. Who are your mentors? What have you learned from them?

A. I came to Colorado in 1983 to attend the Boulder School of Massage Therapy. Back then, you could study almost anything you wished. I wanted to know how people from different cultures got along, healed, and simply walked every day. I began to see that every culture had its own systems, from traditional Chinese medicine doctors to Amazon healers. And they all lived great and terrible lives. They didn't have to be angels to be helpers. I liked this because Spirit is everyone's. It is not a restrictive one God thing.

Only two men taught at the massage school; the rest were women. I knew I had to know my way among men to know my way in the world. It's not a gender comment. Often, women know more of who they are and it's a beautiful reminder. We men can get lost because we are way underestimated and under-allowed.

Tom Daly was one of the men teaching. He was getting his doctorate in ceremonial arts with a specialty in male initiation rights. He asked me to help him do fieldwork. Twenty-five years later, this early mentor is now my dear friend and colleague and I'm still doing fieldwork.

> "Many of us get to the gates of initiation and then go back and turn on the television."

Dr. John Herman was another mentor. In 1910, he was on a coast guard ship that sank and he was its only survivor. From that day, he went and studied with Gandhi and came back to work as a naturopathic physician. Every year, he had dozens of babies dropped off at his doorstep because the women knew their infants would be taken care of. He practiced for seventy-five years and lived until he was 106 years old.

Alice Treadway, the medicine woman I lived with for eleven

days, was also a mentor. She asked me to move through life with a spirit team, a group of human and nonhuman energies such as Lake Superior and my great aunt, who could guide me. I was to renew this team every few years to see who was closest and could come the quickest. I use this team not just when I am in trouble, but also when I'm going to be a part of something larger and I want it to be useful. In some way, working with a spirit team is elemental. For example, if Dr. Herman is with me, *he's* not actually here but *something* is. I have a lot of respect for the strong, serious disciplines but, working with a spirit team is not something you have to earn by suffering for years. It is our birthright. I enjoy helping people create their own teams.

Joanna Macy is another mentor. She is eighty years old and has spent her life helping people who serve others. She is doing amazing work around getting us to feel the grief of the Earth, the cuts we are making, without blaming us, the cutters. She holds a key to the transition we are making from industrialized world to a more compassionate planet. She has been around long enough to get the alchemy, or ingredients, right for sustaining the soup. She also understands that it's not about her. She is just tracking like Joseph Campbell and Marion Woodman.

Other mentors include the poet, Robert Bly, and the mythopoetic men's movement leader, Michael Meade. Meade is doing some of the most creative seed planting for future generations through his work with mythology and ritual.

I am blessed and cursed with these people. Like the Rainer Maria Rilke poem says, "Lay yourself on the slab of my friendship and let my love cut you deep so you'll never forget." There's some cut that's good in being with these people. Each in some way has had to work hard to stay alive, to not give up.

JEFFREY DUVALL

Q. What is the greatest challenge facing society?

A. It is what to do with the energies that move through us, that are part of who we are because of our ancientness—the desire to give birth, make love, wage war, etc. These energies, or archetypes, have been with us for many lifetimes. As a result, they are hard to change. When we do have a choice, we almost always choose the old way, or most of the old way with a little bit of the new. How lost do we have to get in order to be found? How uncomfortable do we need to be? Is war part of the solution? The people who have inspired me felt they had to engage in conflict. Yet, most of us know that violence doesn't work. It's an old tool. So the question becomes, "What would I do if someone were to harm our children, our world?" I want to keep chewing on this mystery.

Because I was around a lot of violence as a boy, I'm extremely sensitized to it. I know it's just as much in me as it is in others. What's underneath that energy is what we're really trying to get at, something that is twenty feet below the Earth's surface. There is something there for us. I don't want to feel shame for what we have done in anger. Shame is like a leaking nuclear reactor. It's poison. But, I do understand reconciliation and feel regret for what has become of the world. In 30,000 years, I'll be curious to see how it goes.

Q. What advice would you give someone just starting his or her spiritual path?

A. Over the years, a lot of people have asked for my advice. One of the first things I say is. "Make *our* time together *yours*. See See me simply as an energy reflecting back what's already inside you and has been working its way out for ten thousand years." I say, especially to youth, "There is great mystery and wonder running through every cell of your body. It is already who you are and is waiting for you to find it. You are no mistake. You have tremendous gifts to give to the world. Learn a discipline that liberates you. Trust and don't hold back. Your life is meant to be played out like a story. It doesn't matter what your career is or what words you use. It's about the wonder you were born with being allowed to run free and barefoot. It's about living the arts, the things that don't have to do with earning a salary and existed before modern technology like answering machines.

Our desire to be stimulated through television and Twitter leave us unable to contemplate long enough to drop down into some sense of knowing, some rooted place. But, young people say to me, "Why should I grow up? Look at the world. I'm never going to get married. I'm never going to be accountable to my children. Why should I do anything but take care of my own selfish needs?" Because our youth have not grown up with authority ("authority" means "guide"), they can trust that when they reach the age they need to be authority, they don't have faith in themselves. Instead, they stay perpetual adolescents in their parents' homes. It's not just youth. Many of us get to the gates of initiation and then go back and turn on the television. We let someone else live our lives and, over time, end up feeling smaller and smaller.

Q. What are your practices for connecting to your higher purpose?
A. Being with my wife and son and witnessing how much they love life. This opens a crack in the door of mystery, wonder, and inspiration. Being outside and reading poetry also heals my soul and sets me free. My work is a way I stay connected because when somebody asks for my support, I have to wake up. I especially like working with young people. I owe it to them because they have something important they brought into this life. I need to listen and be in relationship with them, but not necessarily be their friends. This can be tricky.

I also feel gratitude to my parents, to whom I owe a long thank you. I loved them dearly and they loved me even though we did not know how to show it very well. In some

JEFFREY DUVALL

traditions, they say thank you ten thousand times. I feel this energetic in my body going back at least seven generations, maybe even further than that. It's not that I can do my ancestors' work, but I can give thanks so they know they lived for good reason and that their lives produced something beautiful.

So, there's this continuum, a sense of our place in the world: where we came from, where we are, and where we are going. Quantum physicists tell us nothing ever dies. The same water that is here existed 1½ million years ago. You see this aspen tree? It didn't come here by chance. It began thousands of years ago and is in its right place. Knowing this gives me faith, a sense that we will know what to do to sustain the planet and ourselves. We will know how to love, how to do war that does not destroy, how to be one in our diversity. Even that which we despise we will come to embrace because love and hate are energetically similar. I love to say this to young people because they are so hungry to know that it's not a big mistake. Our suicide rates have quadrupled and are continuing to go up. They need to know there is a purpose to it all.

"Love always works."
Timothy Freke, Best Selling Author and Stand-up Philosopher

Tim Freke is a passionate and entertaining voice for our collective awakening whose enthusiasm for life is contagious. He's clear, irreverent, down-to-earth and not remotely interested in setting himself up as some sort of guru. His controversial books and animated live performances have inspired thousands around the world. Tim has an honors degree in philosophy and is an internationally respected authority on world spirituality. He has spent his life exploring the expanded state of consciousness he calls "the magical mystery experience," "deep awake," and "lucid living" He has a talent for helping others experience this amazing state for themselves.

Tim is the author of over twenty books that have established his reputation as a groundbreaking scholar and freethinker. He is best known for his works on Christian Gnosticism with coauthor Peter Gandy, including *The Jesus Mysteries*, which was a top ten best seller in the U.K. and U.S. and was named Book of the Year by the U.K. *Daily Telegraph*. He is also an innovative stand-up philosopher, a concept he developed from the ancient idea of a philosopher as a traveling spiritual entertainer who transformed people's consciousness. In his mind-blowing stand-up performances and life changing seminars, he shares profound ideas and practical techniques for waking up to oneness and "big love."

Tim is the founder of The Alliance for Lucid Living and is on the board of advisors for Team Humanity, organizations that are dedicated to our collective awakening. He is often featured in documentary films and chat shows broadcast by the BBC, the History Channel and other global media. Tim lives with his wife Debbie and their two children in Glastonbury, England.

TIMOTHY FREKE

Q. What experiences put you on your spiritual path?

A. It all started when I was twelve years old. I was puzzled by life. The grown-ups around me seemed to act as if they knew what it was about, yet it seemed to me that nobody did—that life was a profound mystery. I would sit on a hill with my dog overlooking my hometown and wonder about the great mysteries of existence.

Then one day something happened. I entered a state of consciousness I now think of as being "deep awake." It was as if the world had turned inside out and I discovered a deeper part of me that was one with everything and everyone. It was a moment of recognition that I couldn't put into words. The thing I remember most was that the universe seemed to be permeated with overwhelming love. The experience did not last long and I came down the hill and, in many respects, carried on the life of a teenage boy. Yet something had fundamentally changed. I was looking to experience that deep awake state—that change of consciousness—again. This set me off on a journey in which I have been exploring life, philosophy, and spirituality in search of a route back to that deep awake state. And also to share it with others.

Q. How did these experiences change you?

A. From that experience, I learned something that has stayed with me, which is that love is the most important thing. I call it "big love" because it is an all-embracing, unconditional love. Over the last four decades, everything else has changed. I have developed a sophisticated philosophy of life and written many books. But, fundamentally, the one thing I really know is that love is what matters.

I came down from the hill and wrote a play about what I had realized. It was a big deal in our town. The media came because the play was written and performed by children. The other day I came across it and was astonished to read the

AUTHOR/PHILOSOPHER

last page because it could have been from one of my books now. It's funny to see that although I feel I have changed so much, essentially the message I was interested in communicating at twelve or thirteen is exactly the same today.

Q. What changes are you noticing about your life and the world?

A. I think of this deep awake state as "lucid living" because it is like lucid dreaming. There is really one of us, one awareness, which is dreaming itself to be everything and everyone. When I say the word "dream," I mean it as an analogy. I'm not saying this is literally a dream but that it's like a dream, a collective dream. We are separate within the dream and yet essentially one dreamer. When I am lost in the dream of life, I struggle with being Tim because I think I am just Tim. And it's lonely and scary. But when I am deep awake, I contact the deeper part of myself, which is the dreamer—which is where we are all one. When this happens, I enter the state of lucid living. Then, like in a lucid dream, I see that, paradoxically, I'm both in the dream and the dream is in me. I appear to be Tim, the separate individual in the dream. But really I'm the dreamer, the oneness of awareness, which is not in the dream. That recognition provides a totally different experience of the moment.

Q. What has been the most challenging part of your path?

A. Oh my God, there were so many. The biggest challenge is to live as Tim. As I come to know the deep awake state, there is great relief in disappearing into the presence of oneness and love. And yet I can't stay there. There's still Tim, this separate individual with all his history, quirks, and idiosyncrasies. The continual challenge is coming to terms with Tim and loving him because, like everyone, there are things about myself that I like and don't like. He has a way of being that is different from others. This means there is separation. That Tim is an individual who is separate and will live and die. Being able to embrace this experience is a challenge, but one I'm getting better at as I grow older. I am now fifty years of age.

TIMOTHY FREKE

Q. What is your earliest memory? Why do you remember it?

A. My earliest memory is falling down the stairs when I was two or three years old. We were living in a little flat above my parents' hairdressing business. I remember standing at the top and then falling down the stairs, banging myself about quite nastily. The reason I remember it is because it was quite traumatic. Actually, the only memory I really have is of tottering at the top of the stairs. But, in all honesty, I can't say how much of that is false memory from ideas my parents put into me versus the actual memory itself.

The earliest memory I know is mine is the story I told you about being on the hill when I was twelve. I know that was my own experience, which I held very close and did not share.

Q. Who are your mentors? What have you learned from them?

A. I've had many teachers. Some taught me through books. Others I spent time with. Ram Das had a big influence on me at one point. So did Ramesh Balsekar, an Indian teacher I met. But the person who has been my greatest teacher is my mom. I don't say that lightly. My mother is the most extraordinary being. She embodies much of what I have come to understand about the way to live. She reads my books and is interested, but she's not philosophical. She sees herself as an ordinary woman. She's in her eighties now, has had cancer three times, a bleed on the brain, and God knows what else. Yet she is totally effervescent with life. She gives constantly in a totally unselfconscious way.

A few years back, I was running a retreat for people who were dying. My mother volunteered to feed the group. I remember seeing her come in and out of the room, cleaning up. Then it struck me like a thunderbolt. I had been running around the world looking for enlightened masters to teach me and the person who could teach me the most about being of service was my mom. She had been there the whole time and was so close I hadn't noticed.

When she got cancer the first time, I wrote a song for her called, "Famous Amongst Angels." In this world, the famous are celebrities, politicians, and pop stars. I liked the idea that the angels have never heard of any of these people. But the angels know all about those completely unnoticed people like my mother who are naturally alive, good, and filled with love. My mom is a massive inspiration to me.

Q. What is the greatest challenge facing society?

A. Our greatest challenge is to wake up from the illusion of separateness, which sounds very abstract but it isn't. When we believe we are separate, we exploit each other and nature. If we can understand that we are one with everything then all that changes. With the oneness comes big love. It's that love which can lead to the transformation of human consciousness. That love and oneness can set our creativity free.

Because we humans are extremely creative, it's just a matter of what we use that creativity for. If we wake up to oneness, then we can use it to solve the world's problems—all of them. And if we don't, then we'll just go on creating more problems. But I'm an optimist because I think the evolution of consciousness is moving towards oneness. I don't think it's going to happen tomorrow, but I think we are moving in that direction. We are part of a slow, spluttering evolution toward something better.

Q. What advice would you give someone just starting his or her spiritual path?

A. What I offer people is a way to become conscious of our deeper identity, which is one with everything, and celebrate our separate identity, which is living out its life in the life dream. I take people on a journey into the magical mystery of life where we feel how extraordinary it is to experience

TIMOTHY FREKE

the wonder of existence. It's the experience I had on the hill, which is beyond words but can't be missed when you have it. And it doesn't stop there. Then it's about how to take that experience into ordinary life. I am a father who has all the everyday struggles any parent has. For me, it's about honoring and loving this dream of separateness from the recognition of our essential oneness. That's what I have been exploring all my life and that's what I've been able to help others explore.

Q. What are your practices for connecting to your higher purpose?

A. There are many I do, which I explore in my latest book, *How Long is Now?* The most important is to enter the mystery of existence, which I discovered by accident when I was twelve on the hill. When I woke up this first time, I didn't know what had happened. For years I thought it had come about spontaneously. More recently, it dawned on me that I had profoundly entered the mystery of the moment. So if I get caught up in the story of Tim—my dramas, worries, and so on—the thing that sets me free most quickly is to stop and bring my attention to the present. Then I realize that I have no idea what's going on. The truth is, I know nothing.

When I confront the mystery of my existence, then I am face-to-face with the reality of the moment and it is so profoundly mysterious, I can't begin to grasp it. Suddenly my story dissolves and I'm there in the awesome, breathtaking mystery. Then I can approach my story from a new perspective because I have just stepped out of it. Not knowing is what always wakes me up.

Q. How do you use these practices when you get out of balance, like when your kids get upset?

A. Remembering that you don't know is important as a parent. But it's also important to be able to enter into life with your kids as they experience it. I connect with that deeper part of

AUTHOR/PHILOSOPHER

myself, which is always a child. That oceanic presence that you see in babies, which is the same now as when we were born. I also connect with Tim, the fifty-year-old man who is in the world, because what my children want is for me to be both a child and a responsible adult—both in the moment and in time. From that place, I can meet them in whatever they are confronting and, at the same time, be a responsible parent who takes care of them.

Q. How do you resolve the paradox that we are already every-thing we seek yet we still have a mission to fulfill on Earth?

A. The big insight for me is the concept of polarity. The whole of life is made up of polarities—one and many, good and bad, male and female, day and night, life and death, and on and on it goes. The mistake we make is thinking that the answer to these profound questions is either/or. Is it about planning or going with the flow? Is it about knowing we are all one or actualizing ourselves as individuals? My experience points towards the solution being both/and, that it's both about waking up to my essential nature as oneness and about ac-tualizing my individual nature as a separate person. Tim, my separate identity, is a responsible adult who lives in time and must do a certain amount of planning. But, my deeper iden-tity is not planning anything. It's just in the moment—look-ing, watching, and appreciating everything as it unfolds.

When I'm lucid, I experience both of these, whereas if I am just Tim, I become anxious because I can't actually control life. On the other hand, if I just go into the spacious empti-ness, then my ordinary life can start to dissolve. That would be great if I lived in a cave in the Himalayas but it isn't any good as a parent and someone doing a job.

But it's not an either/or question. I can be in both places at once. I can engage with the opposites inherent in life, both planning and going with the flow, thinking logically and being intuitive. I can allow Tim to play out his everyday roles and,

TIMOTHY FREKE

at the same time, I can be conscious of my deeper identity, which is here in the moment enjoying my life like a movie.

Q. If you received £100,000, how would you spend it?

A. I'd say, "Thank you but that's not enough." You can't do anything with £100,000 these days. There was a time in my life when I would have given it away to some worthy cause. Now that I'm getting older, my first priority is to honor Tim's separateness as a father and use it to make my family secure. Having done that, I would ask, "How can I use this creatively to bring good ideas into the world?" I'm a philosopher. That's what I do with all my money. So first I'm there to make my family secure. That's honoring my separate identity. Then it's about being of service by bringing ideas, love, and awakening as best I can. I would love to have as many resources as possible to introduce these concepts in interesting and innovative ways.

I'd like to see a big multimedia wake-up show involving the best of the arts and stand-up philosophy, which is philosophy as entertainment. I would love to get that off the ground and bring these ideas, which exist in a spiritual ghetto right now, into the mainstream and see what happens.

Q. If you had thirty seconds with someone in an elevator, what three things would you tell him or her to do to be joyful, peaceful, and whole?

A. The insight that came when I worked with people who were dying is that when someone really needs help, words often are not the answer. If I had said my philosophy when working with people facing death or bereavement, it would have fallen from my mouth like a brick. What was happening was too powerful for that. But what I discovered is that love always works. And love doesn't have to be spoken. You can just connect and be with people in that big space. And by doing so, things often change in their consciousness. So in this situation, I would probably say nothing. But I would be as conscious as possible so I could really connect and be with them.

Q. What books or resources have helped you the most? Why?

A. I'm nervous about recommending books because it's a very personal thing. What I can say are the books that have influenced me, which may be of value to others. The key ones are: *The Tao Te Ching*, by Lao Tzu, *I Am That*, by Sri Nisargadatta Maharaj, *How Can I Help?* by Ram Dass and Paul Gorman, *Leaves of Grass,* by Walt Whitman, and *Four Quartets*, by T.S. Eliot. Oh, there are so many. I also think movies can take you to a very interesting place. Films like *The Matrix* or *Field of Dreams* can open up profound insights into the nature of reality.

Q. What do you think of the concept that my enemy is my lover?

A. I much prefer it to "my lover is my enemy," which is the way it can easily end up if we fall asleep into separateness and lose touch with big love!

Q. What would you like to be written on your tombstone?

A. There's a naughty line in *The Gospel of the Second Coming*, a satirical book of philosophy I wrote with my lifelong friend Peter Gandy, which I think would be fun on my tombstone: "DEATH IS COMING, LIFE IS FOREPLAY"

TIMOTHY FREKE

"In dream you love some and not others. On waking up you find you are love itself, embracing all."
- Sri Nisargadatta Maharaj

Reprinted from I Am That (1990) by Sri Nisargadatta Maharaj with permission of The Acorn Press, Durham, NC.

"It's all divine all the time."
Laurie Grant, Kahuna of Oneness and ARCH Founder

Laurie Grant discovered her metaphysical and healing abilities thirty-seven years ago when she spontaneously began getting clear, accurate premonitions. She mastered her gifts and, in 1980, began teaching psychic awareness classes and offering personal consultations, including channeled readings by the Source, hypnotherapy, past life therapy, art therapy, and Reiki. During this time, Laurie directed three holistic health centers, served as a medical intuitive for physicians and other health professionals, and became a New Age television and radio personality, appearing as the featured speaker at national health expos. In 2000, Laurie rediscovered the healing tradition of ancient Hawaiian times, which is called Ancient Rainbow Conscious Healing (ARCH). Laurie now focuses on writing books and teaching workshops to assist people in developing their intuitive and healing abilities for spiritual growth. In 2003, Laurie spontaneously went into a state of oneness non-duality, which the Buddhists call "The Highest Level of Enlightenment." In this state, Laurie is privileged to see beyond the illusion of separation to experience us all as one. Laurie has a master's degree in art therapy and is a kahuna, hypnotherapist, and reiki master teacher. She also has studied acupressure, oriental medicine, tai chi, qigong, massage, and yoga.

Q What experiences put you on your spiritual path?

A. I grew up dyslexic in a family of PhDs. This circumstance forced me to use my intuition to get through school and earn a master's degree. When I was twenty, I started receiving accurate premonitions, e.g., my boyfriend's uncle having a fatal heart attack, my acquaintances getting into a car accident, etc. Since these insights were mostly negative, I tried to erase them from my mind. When I couldn't, I sought guidance from psychics. The first one said this intuitive gift was my destiny. I would use it to teach thousands of people around the world. The second one taught me how to control it so it did not control me.

Q. How did these experiences change you?

A. As I opened my sixth sense, I started connecting with Divine Source and progressed from being psychic to being spiritual. From Divine Source, I began channeling information to help individuals with health and other concerns. The doctors I worked with said I had near 100% accuracy in diagnosing their tough cases. I ended up being booked a year in advance for body readings two decades before Caroline Myss coined the term medical intuition. The privilege of accessing higher levels of consciousness to help change people's lives taught me to live in faith rather than fear.

Q. What changes are you noticing about your life and the world?

A. Having the stigmata, the crucifixion wounds of Jesus, came as the biggest shock. I initially had no idea what to do. I just wanted to make it stop. Then, when I went into the state of oneness non-duality, I realized we are all one—with the divine and each other. I now share these experiences to help people awaken to our oneness. These experiences also helped me honor oneness in everyone, including my supposed enemies. For example, in the past, I had been critical of George W. Bush and how he ran our country. Now I have great compassion for him and the divine purpose he served in setting us up for great change. The world is moving to a higher level of consciousness. On June 20, 2008, the Earth aligned with the core of the universe and light and energy emissions hit our planet. Since then, there has been more and more interest in living in oneness and going green.

Q. What changes are others noticing about you?

A. My children love and accept me. However, the more conscious I become, the more invincible they see me as being.

For example, my daughters recently saw a YouTube video in which I bless people and they pass out in bliss. Their response was, "Yeah mom, isn't that what you do?" Similarly, my daughter once called me from school wanting two juices with lunch. She said, "Mom, tell my teachers that I want two. They will do what you say." I replied, "No, honey they won't. You get only one juice with lunch." These situations are tough because my kids really believe I can do anything. My ex-husband, on the other hand, wasn't meant to handle the changes and moved on. In general, I think my family would say I have become even more loving, tolerant, and compassionate.

Q. What has been the most challenging part of your path?

A. Knowing things about people before they are ready to acknowledge them. This challenge is hardest with my children. I knew my oldest daughter's life lesson when she was five but recognized it was hers to learn. I can only give her tools. My hope is that she learns her lesson the most graceful way possible. I extend this same grace to all people learning their lessons. It helps me accept people where they are.

Q. What is your earliest memory? Why do you remember it?

A. When I was three, I had an invisible playmate named Dobbin. Despite my mother's protests, I insisted Dobbin was real. I now realize that he was one of my early guides. When I was eight, two other guides came to support me through my parent's divorce. They looked like aliens and one was named Gibby Gail.

Q. Who are your mentors? What have you learned from them?

A. Twenty years ago, the water got shut off at a hotel at which I was teaching. The other hotel guests and I went across the street to get something to eat at a diner. As I sat at the diner's counter, a man came in and said to the cook, "We need to shut your water off for the next four hours." Instead of panicking, the woman replied, "Okay, but first fill all the

LAURIE GRANT

buckets you can find with water." Then she returned to her singing and cooking. Most people would have panicked with a restaurant full of people and no running water. She didn't. Instead, she chose the best option available and life went on. Her response is a model for how to deal with life's challenges. The Dalai Lama also is an inspiration in how he handles his role and lives in peace, regardless of what goes on in the world. Gandhi, too, had great impact on me.

Q. What is the greatest challenge facing society?

A. Fear is the greatest challenge. Spiritual leaders often advise us to ignore or let go of it. However, our parents inadvertently programmed fear into our bodies to keep us safe. Since it is there, we must acknowledge and address it. We can do this by saying, "Fear, thank you for your concern. I understand you are trying to keep me safe. But right now, I ask that you step aside because I can handle this situation. I promise if I need you, I will call on you." When people learn to acknowledge their fears, open their hearts, and live in faith, we'll have a more peaceful planet.

Q. What advice would you give someone just starting his or her spiritual path?

A. Get quiet and tune in to your intuition. It's like a muscle. The more you use it, the stronger it will become. Use your extra sensory perception (ESP) learning style to access it. If you are visual, notice what you see. If you are auditory, notice what you hear. If you are kinesthetic, notice what you feel. If you are knowing, notice what thoughts come to mind. You don't have to know how your intuition works—just like you don't have to know how your television works—you just have to tune in. In prehistoric times, we used our intuition to find food, shelter, etc. Now, we rely on GPS systems and road signs to guide us. However, there is more information available than the mind can comprehend. CEOs understand this concept. They score high on ESP tests because they often combine intellect and intuition to make sound business decisions. Opening up your intuition will automatically lead you along your spiritual path.

Q. What are your practices for connecting to your higher purpose?

A. Living in Maui allows me to spend time in nature sitting on a rock, wading in a stream, walking on the beach, and watching the sunset. Sometimes I look at the intricacies of a flower and marvel at the divine force at work in the world. This force is beyond what we can perceive with our five senses. In Hawaiian, the Divine Source is called "Ke Akua."

My latest practice started on February 1st when the Cosmic Mother appeared to me and asked, "Do you remember what you were told in your near death experience?" I replied, "Yes, I was surrounded by unconditional love and I asked if I could send it to my children. Then I heard, "They are all your children. Go back and remind them of who they are." "I understand the remind part but am unclear on what all my children means," I replied. She responded, "Would you be willing to commit to loving everyone as a mother loves her child?" to which I answered, "Yes, of course, if it is my kuleana," (the Hawaiian word for privilege and responsibility). At that moment, she came into me and I became her embodiment. Hers is the healing energy I send out to every living being during morning and evening prayer. This energy helps awaken the world to divine oneness. Ironically, right after this sacred event, she led me to Wal-Mart, where I performed a darshan, a blessing to give people divine vision. Wal-Mart was completely transformed.

> "The more we live in faith, the less drama (trauma) we need to learn our lessons."

Q. How do you use these practices when you get out of balance?

A. Since I live in faith rather than fear, I stay balanced most of the time. However, I am human so there are occasions when balance doesn't come as naturally. When this happens, I center myself by standing on the Earth, in the sand or grass. I also go into servitude, asking to be led by the Spirit, rather than my personality, which may not choose as wisely. For example, every morning I ask, "How may I serve today?" The Cosmic Mother then leads me to people who need "light help." Since I spend a lot of time in airports, I bless the people I meet, helping them awaken to higher levels of consciousness. They don't always know what I am doing but they do feel their divine self enliven.

> "Get quiet and tune in to your intuition. It's like a muscle. The more you use it, the stronger it will become."

Q. How do you balance planning with remaining open to opportunity?

A. I allow the Cosmic Mother to lead me, trusting that it is all divine all the time. When challenges arise, I see them as opportunities to learn lessons and live in mastery. The more we live in faith, the less drama (trauma) we need to learn our lessons. Also, flexibility helps, especially when it comes to our children. We must trust the divine plan guiding their lives even when we cannot know all of it.

Q. If you received $100,000, how would you spend it?

A. I would open a healing center where my students could give efficient, effective treatments to people led to come. I would continue my global healing work while coordinating the center's activities and compensating the students for their services.

Q. If you had thirty seconds with someone in an elevator, what three things would you tell the person to do to be joyful, peaceful, and whole?

KAHUNA OF ONENESS

A. First, I would give the person a blessing. I would tell him or her that what s/he is feeling is his or her true divine self. The more s/he honors this place of divinity, the more s/he can live in a higher state of consciousness. When I do a blessing, I am not adding anything. I only awaken the divine already present in the person and, for that, no additional words are needed.

Q. What books or resources have helped you the most? Why?

A. I have a book coming out called, *Transform Your Life NOW! The Spiritual KEY to Excelling in These Times.* People will be drawn to this work if it is right for them. Everybody has his or her own way of awakening to divine oneness. For some, it will be through Buddhism or Christianity; for others, it will be through nature or no path at all. Consequently, there is no one book or resource that fits everyone. Ask your guidance to lead you to the words of wisdom you seek.

Q. What would you like to be written on your tombstone?

A. I'm going to be cremated and have my ashes scattered in the ocean. If I had a tombstone it would say, "It's all divine all the time." I want to be remembered as having honored the divine in everyone. My greatest life lesson has been learning that I can't honor in others what I don't honor in myself. So, by honoring the divine in me, I can now awaken the divine in all I touch.

Q. Anything else?

A. Many people ask me, "What is it like to experience oneness non-duality?" Unlike near death experiences, which differ based on a person's faith, oneness encounters are all the same.

> "Enlightenment is not endarkenment. It is meant to be radiant, fun, and blissful as we become one with everything in the universe."

They are characterized by an overwhelming feeling of bliss

LAURIE GRANT

as the person loses his or her sense of a physical body, sense of time, and motivation to do anything other than remain in oneness. Now I experience everything as part of the divine matrix and find myself giggling in airplanes when I realize they are just balls of energy hurling through the sky.

My main mission in life is to remind everyone that whether you believe it or not, you are the divine all the time! According to psychiatrist David Hawkins, only one in ten million people go into oneness non-duality. However, we don't have to wait thousands of lifetimes for one in ten million to go into this state. We can encourage ourselves to wake up by going within and expanding our consciousness. As we do, we will realize that enlightenment is not endarkenment. It is meant to be radiant, fun, and blissful as we become one with everything in the universe.

In the summer of 2007, I went to India and stayed among divine beings living in this state. The level of oneness I went into left me no longer needing sleep and able to do divine transmissions. So I now remain conscious all the time. Although it was tempting to stay in India in this amazing state of bliss, I knew it was my kuleana (privilege and responsibility) to return home to help others awaken to oneness.

KAHUNA OF ONENESS

"There is a certain uncertainty that we need to have."
Rev. Dr. Kent Ira Groff, Oasis Ministries

Kent Ira Groff is a spiritual companion for journeyers and leaders, as well as a writer and retreat leader living in Denver, Colorado. He describes his work as "one beggar showing other beggars where to find bread." You can travel with Kent through his books: *Active Spirituality: A Guide for Seekers and Ministers*; *Journeymen: A Spiritual Guide for Men*; *The Soul of Tomorrow's Church*; *What Would I Believe if I Didn't Believe Anything?: A Handbook for Spiritual Orphans*; *Writing Tides: Finding Grace and Growth through Writing*, and; *Facing East, Praying West* (2010). He serves as founding mentor of Oasis Ministries, Camp Hill, PA, and leads seminars at retreat centers, campuses, theological seminaries, and faith communities in the U.S. and abroad.

Q. What experiences put you on your spiritual path?
A. At age five, I asked my mother what I should be when I grew up: a minister, a carpenter, or a farmer. My mother replied in reverse order, first considering farmer, then carpenter, then minister. I knew that going into the ministry was a way off the farm. When I thought about the ministry, I imagined a square church with a square pulpit. After twenty years of this approach, I now have a round church with a round pulpit—the world is my church.

Q. How did these experiences change you?
A. When life gets tangled, you walk away, you let it go. If it comes back, it comes as a gift. I first realized this when my daughter—2 ½ years old at the time—got her new kite hopelessly snagged in a tree. We were about to leave when I gen-

tly tugged on the kite and it miraculously came free. I had this experience again when I left my parish and received back the ministry in a new form—chaplaincy, spiritual formation at the Shalem Institute, and the creation of Oasis Ministries. What got me through the conflict and uncertainty of that time was a sermon on St. John of the Cross, and his treatise, *Dark Night of the Soul*.

Q. What has been the most challenging part of your path?

A. The most challenging part was thrusting myself into the void after leaving parish ministry and not knowing where it would take me. In the span of a year and a half, I met a Jesuit spiritual director, heard about the Shalem Institute, and founded Oasis Ministries. Forming Oasis Ministries was a very big challenge and we just celebrated our twentieth anniversary! One of the qualities I'm writing about in a book on aging is resiliency—to ability to bounce back like Jesus' crucifixion and resurrection. Nothing can keep you down if you have the resiliency to rebound with compassion and gratitude.

Q. What changes are you noticing about your life and the world?

A. Spiritual people often think they should feel complete joy and happiness. Joy is different from happiness, which is about happenstance that comes and goes. A story told by German Theologian, Helmut Thielicke, illustrates this distinction best. During World War II, Thielicke was preaching to his congregation when bombs started going off overhead. As the congregation sought shelter under the pews, someone began singing, *"Jesu, Mein Freude"* ("Jesus My Joy"). The sound was so dissonant that giggling erupted—holy laughter—amidst the violence. We're given these moments of paradox to relieve life's intensity.

Q. What changes are others noticing about you?

A. That I'm different, a creative, outside-the-box thinker. I pay a lot of attention to dreams and enjoy playing with words. In the early 1990s, I had a dream that my computer caught

OASIS MINISTRIES

on fire and I tried to dowse it, but the flames would not go out. My spiritual director, a sister of the Immaculate Heart of Mary said, "Sounds like the burning bush to me." The computer represented my writing, which later became my pulpit. I put a dictionary at the top of the stairs to encourage my children to fall in love with words, as I had. I hear three words in nearly every conversation: I love you. These three words are worth all the dictionaries.

Q. What is your earliest memory? Why do you remember it?
A. I remember my mother quickly covering me in the bathtub when the bread man came to our house with a delivery. This early memory of shame later sparked my interest in a passage in the Gospel of Mark, 14:52. In the passage, a youth following Jesus wearing only a linen cloth is stripped naked by the guards and runs away. In Mark 16:4, we find a youth seated at the right side of the tomb wearing a white robe. This youth's reappearance symbolizes being stripped naked, crucified, and rising in Christ to be clothed in kindness, love, and compassion.

When I left the parish ministry and became a chaplain, I was that youth, stripped of the church's status, with a naked intent for God alone. If I could do it again, I would pull off that towel and show the bread man the whole thing!

Q. Who are your mentors? What have you learned from them?
A. Bruce Metzger, my thesis advisor and New Testament Professor at Princeton. I went to see him halfway through the school year because I was not sure I could finish my thesis. Bruce encouraged me by meeting with me a few minutes every week. His support resulted in my completing the thesis and winning the thesis prize! From this experience, I learned that mentoring does not need to take a lot of time. Brief encounters and encouragement are all that is needed.
Other mentors include:

Rev. Dr. Kent Ira Groff

John Oliver Nelson, founder of the Kirkland Retreat Center, who helped me form Oasis Ministries. Even though he's passed away, he's still with me.

Diogenes Allen, spiritual formation professor at Princeton, who introduced me to writers such as Blaise Pascal, Simone Weil, and Søren Kierkegaard and encouraged me to write for both lay people and scholars when editors told me I couldn't.

Mary Jean Irion, founder of Chautauqua's Writer's Center, who encouraged me so much in my writing.

Q. What is the greatest challenge facing society?

A. Poverty and war. Why not teach peace negotiations in the same hard-nosed fashion that we teach military strategy? We have recent examples of nonviolent change, e.g., South Africa, the former Soviet Union, the Berlin Wall's collapse. Poverty and religious extremism contribute to war, pitting insiders against outsiders. In James 1:19, it says, "You must understand this, my beloved: let everyone be quick to listen, slow to speak, and slow to anger." It's the inability to say, "I may not be right," that really causes war. There is a certain uncertainty we need to have.

Teaching how to listen is an important part of my work. I compare it to this tree [pointing to a tree]. The tree's roots represent listening beneath the surface of life, its branches are communication or action, and the trunk in between is *Shema*, or contemplation. So, contemplation goes both ways. It's contemplating the inner life and the outer world. If we can teach contemplative listening, then we can affect our political structures. One of the ways I work for peace is writing. The pen is mightier than the sword.

Q. What advice would you give someone just starting his or her spiritual path?

A. Pray always and in all ways. Pray always is to be continually in

OASIS MINISTRIES

prayer. Pray all ways is to pray using different forms of prayer. We can do anything as a prayer: take a walk, light a candle, etc. In doing so, we get rid of the sacred-secular split, as contemplation and action happen simultaneously. As Gandhi said, "My life is my message."

I heard the Bishop of Liverpool say that the son of man is Adam, which means "earth." So, Jesus, the most divine being, is the child of earth. This idea of heaven and earth coming together is fundamental to our lives becoming prayer. As in the Lord's Prayer, thy will be done on Earth as it is in heaven.

Q. What are your practices for connecting to your higher purpose?

A. I "backed" into my prayer exercises because my spine has been my Achilles' heel since birth. As with Paul, my weak place also is my strength. Each morning, I do back exercises, which become prayers as I count repetitions using the Lord's Prayer. When I finish, I walk to the park and pray in the four (really six) directions—East (youth), South (vocation), West (letting go), and North (death and a sense of direction). I pray for everyone who lives each way, do tai chi, finish my walk, and return home to meditate on the word. I also journal, starting each entry with thank you in different languages: *gracias* (Spanish), *mahalo* (Hawaiian), and *xie xie* (Chinese). Then I meditate on something for which I am grateful. Often I'll write about my dreams, draft a poem, or draw a picture, such as this church burning [pointing to a picture of a church]. I wrote this next to it, "Let the church catch fire with joy and passion. Existing forms may need to be consumed for new ones to be born."

Q. How do you use these practices when you get out of balance?

A. I snapped at my wife this morning when she suggested something that I thought wouldn't work. I noticed what I'd done, caught my breath, and decided I didn't need to respond that way. I use the centering prayer word *amor*, which means love in different romance languages, to return to balance. I tell my students to pray intentionally so that when they are in an intense situation, they'll pray unconsciously because they've bathed themselves in love, gratitude, and compassion. I also have a singing bowl near my computer. Sometimes I'll stop work, strike it, and listen to its sound before reengaging. It softens the edges.

Q. How do you balance planning with remaining open to opportunity?

A. I have a prayer that says, "Make a plan, give up a plan." When Jesus met the Canaanite woman, he knew he was sent to only the lost sheep of Israel, not to the gentile Canaanites. Her persistence in saying, "Yes, Lord, but even the dogs feed on the crumbs, which fall from their master's table," changed his plan and enlarged Jesus' circle to include gentiles.

With writing, "It's make an outline, give up an outline." If the outline returns, let it be your friend and not your master. My favorite poem is one I wrote when I couldn't think of anything to write: "I write about nothing / No thing / No thing that really matters / Only relationships." I wrote about nothing and, in a few lines, I ended up with everything. Even scientists will tell you, matter is just relationships.

Q. If you received $100,000, how would you spend it?

A. The resources would go toward teaching the art of listening, alleviating poverty, and fostering peace. Listening is crucial to peacemaking and prosperity. So a large piece would go to Oasis Ministries, another part to Bono's global www.one.org, and the last part, to local Habit for Humanity projects and my family.

Q. If you had thirty seconds with someone in an elevator, what three things would you tell the person to do to be joyful, peaceful, and whole?

A. From Godspell, ". . . to see thee more clearly, to love thee more dearly, to follow thee more nearly." First, we become aware or mindful. This is the beginning of all spiritual and scientific life. In fact, being aware is the essence of everything. Then, we grow in compassion or love, which is at the heart of all traditions. Finally, we follow our bliss into the world of action.

Q. What books or resources have helped you the most? Why?

A. Classics. These mystic authors experienced glimpses of God. Julian of Norwich, Meister Eckhart, George Herbert (Poetry), and John of the Cross; all Library of Christian Classics titles; Søren Kierkegaard, *Fear and Trembling*, *Works of Love*, and *Attack Upon Christendom*; Pascal, *Pensées*; Simone Weil, *Waiting for God*; Henri J.M. Nouwen, *The Wounded Healer*; Evelyn Underhill, *The Spiritual Life*; Brother Lawrence, *The Practice of the Presence of God*; Thomas Merton, *New Seeds of Contemplation*; Dietrich *Bonhoeffer*, *Life Together* and *The Cost of Discipleship*; Fyodor Dostoyevsky, *The Brothers Karamazov*; Leo Tolstoy, *War and Peace*; *The Essential Gandhi*, ed. Louis Fischer; *The Journals of John Woolman*; Howard Thurman, *Jesus and the Disinherited*, *A Strange Freedom* and *For the Inward Journey*; Teresa of Avila, *The Interior Castle*; Thomas a Kempis, *The Imitation of Christ*, ed. Wm. Creasey; Victor Hugo, *Les Miserables*; Albert Schweitzer, *The Quest of the Historical Jesus*.

Contemporary. Especially fiction. Fiction gets us to see ourselves and the divine in ways direct spiritual writing can't. Sue Monk Kidd, *The Secret Life of Bees*, *When the Heart Waits*; Rachael Naomi Remen, *Kitchen Table Wisdom*; Kathleen Norris, *Dakota: A Spiritual Geography*; The stories of Flannery O'Connor; Raymond Carver's short stories; The stories of John Cheever; Robert Bly, Iron John; Joseph Campbell, *The Power of Myth*; Annie Dillard, *The Writing Life and Pilgrim at Tinker Creek*; Strunk and White, *Elements of Style* and White's *Charlotte's Web*.

Poetry. Poetry creates a holistic and primal way of praying, drawing on intuition, imagination, and intellect to respond to God's grace. *The Collected Poems* of Langston Hughes; Walt Whitman, *Leaves of Grass* and prose sorks; Gerard Manley Hopkins, *Immortal Diamond*; Denise Levertov, *Sands of the Well*; Mary Oliver, *New and Selected Poems*; Rainer Maria Rilke, *The Book of Hours* and *Letters to a Young Poet*; *The Rag and Bone Shop of the Heart*. Poets like Yeats, William Carlos Williams, Blake, Dickinson, Neruda, Wallace Stevens, William Stafford; Wendell Berry, Selected Poems.

Films. Films bring people into moments that capture life's grace and confront us with our sacred selves. *The Shawshank Redemption, A River Runs Through It, Babette's Feast, To Kill a Mockingbird, Seabiscuit, Simon Birch, Whaler Rider, Les Miserables, Schindler's List*.

Q. What would you like to be written on your tombstone?

A. The word thanks in many different languages. Meister Eckhart said, "If the only prayer you say in your life is 'thank you,' that would suffice." Gratitude is the root of compassion.

Q. Anything else?

A. The transformation of brokenness into blessing is central to my spirituality. For me, Jesus the Christ is the epitome and essence of this transformation. It's a way of speaking about resiliency, the mystery that after plummeting, we rise again with compassion and gratitude—like the Buddhist sutra, or lotus, which grows out of the trash, or Jesus' crucifixion on the town garbage heap, Golgotha. Wherever I witness this transforming mystery in Muslim, Jewish, or even atheistic people, I see the Christic experience. This way of seeing is how I maintain my unique Christian faith in relation to universal spiritual truth. The "universal way" is the way of dying to what is false and rising to what is real, regardless of faith tradition.

"Are your lights on or off?"
Cathy and Gary Hawk, Clarity International

Cathy Hawk is Founding Director of Clarity International®, a coaching and training firm that teaches skills for how to see, sense, and use energy as a primary life and work strategy. Cathy's innovative Lights on Learning Method™ rapidly connects clients to their purpose, propelling them into action that supports their vision. Since 1994, Cathy and her Clarity trained coaches have guided thousands of leaders, entrepreneurs, and others to find and follow their callings. Her clients include MBS Property Group, Watership Trading Company, Stratecon, Shields Bay & Printing, The Tauri Group, Inn on the Creek Foods, Floating Feather Spa, Soundings on the Planet, Cultivating Connections, New Dimensions Radio, and Institute of Noetic Sciences. As a veteran coach, Cathy's own search for a new vision nearly twenty years ago led to the development of Clarity International® and the Lights on Learning Method™.

Gary Hawk is Managing Director of Clarity International®. He serves as an executive coach and mentor for CEOs, business owners, and senior executives. With over forty years of business experience, Gary's rich background enables him to guide clients in clarifying business and personal goals, and the process for achieving them. Gary is an attorney and served as General Counsel for a producer and syndicator of television commercials, as well as a rapidly growing plastics manufacturer. He also ran the franchise division of a $450 million services company and owned a four-unit chain of weight loss studios. Gary has worked with businesses such as Anadarko, Aradiant, Biogen-Idec, Corporate Express, Encana. Hewlett-Packard, Goal Financial, Lockheed Martin, Maxim Pharmaceuticals, Paychex, Precision Engine Controls, Qualcomm, San Diego Airport Authority, Shamir Insight, Tenet Healthcare, and Towers Perrin.

Q. Can you please tell us about Clarity International's coaching method?

Cathy People in our culture are taught to do everything until they get exhausted and burn out. Many of their activities drain them because they do what others want, rather than what brings them joy. Our lights on coaching approach is counter-cultural. We encourage people to do what they love, what lights them up, and to let go of anything draining. In our book, *Creating the Rest of Your Life*, we guide people through Clarity's Lights on Learning Method© to help them feel the difference between what gives them energy (lights on) and what depletes them (lights off). This discernment helps them take right action.

When I coach people, I actually videotape them before and after our chakra-based interview so they can see this difference and use it as a guide. For example, before pictures often show right-left brain imbalances (appear as left-right face discrepancies), restricted expression (squinted eyes or tight throats), and energy depletion (pale skin or dullness in energy field), all of which improve after the interview.

When a person has a lights on thought, his or her body releases feel good hormones—endorphins like serotonin—which are energizing. This beneficial response causes the person to reflect radiance to the world. He or she looks, feels, and acts differently, causing him or her to attract what he or she wants in life. Conversely, when an individual has a lights off thought, stress-related hormones like cortisol are released, robbing him or her of energy. The person then reflects and acts in a way that attracts what he or she does not want. So, the choice is simple: Are your lights on or off? If what you want to do ranks 7.5 or higher on a 1 to 10 scale, go for it! Your lights are on. If it ranks lower, then change direction. You have to know what lights you up before you can jump into the river of how it will manifest.

Q. What experiences put you on your spiritual path?

Gary In 1994, I began leading peer groups for CEOs and business owners and eventually became a Certified Professional Coach. During this time, I began studying how my thoughts influenced my reality. I undertook this self-study to gain some answers on how to live my life differently than I had been. This led to several years of spiritual study. When I met Cathy, her Lights On Learning Method™ made sense to me. She had packaged much of what I had learned in Religious Science into an easy to use methodology.

Cathy After finishing my first career, I took a sabbatical to study energy medicine, applied kinesiology, and other techniques that show how our thoughts affect our bodies. I integrated these approaches into coaching to help clients find activities that energized or lit them up. I started developing a language to explain these positive physiological changes. I created a river to pictorially represent the flow people navigate to live in an energized, lights on way. I referred to their bodies as human operating systems or internal GPS' that keep them on the right course. I encouraged them to use these systems when they experienced destiny amnesia to find their way home. As a result of this work, my clients began calling me a permissionary, someone who asked them to give themselves permission to follow their calling. After appearing on National Public Radio's *New Dimensions*, I received hundreds of calls from people who said, "You gave me words to describe what I've always known to be true." Science has shown how endorphins are released when people do things they enjoy and, in recent years, how continued focus on doing what they love actually creates new neural pathways in the brain. This validates the behavioral changes I have observed in my clients for years.

CATHY AND GARY HAWK

Q. How did these experiences change you?

Gary   Before I met Cathy, "Change your thoughts, change your life," had an intellectual and spiritual appeal to me but I had not been able to bring these spiritual concepts into my life. Her rapid discovery, rapid recovery method helped me shift my thoughts out of shadow behavior and reclaim my energy. To shift your energy with rapid discovery, rapid recovery you become more aware of where your thoughts are in that moment and consciously switch to a more effective thought and behavior. Esther and Jerry Hicks talk about "sending out the rockets of desire." For example, when I can't connect to the big picture, I still can do something small to energize me and help me operate above the line. From there, I can reflect, look, feel, act, and attract what I desire.

Cathy   I go one level deeper to say, "Change your thoughts, change your physiology." Our physiology is our reality. When our lights are on, our neurological pathways shower us with beneficial hormones, like serotonin. When our lights are off, stress related hormones, like cortisol, drain our energy. So I continually monitor my body to discern whether my lights are on or off. If they are off, I shift my focus to what lights me up. For example, I'll go for a walk, look at a painting, or listen to music. When people fail to develop their internal GPS, or human operating system, they resign themselves to being drained. Eventually, the body creates a crisis to get attention.

Q. What changes are you noticing about your life and the world?

Gary   Before Clarity, I would have become stuck in draining thoughts about the recent economic downturn. Now I accept the new current reality and use Clarity's tools to take steps toward creating a new vision for what I want. As I do, my family and work relationships improve because I reflect clear energy and intention back to the world.

Cathy Keeping my lights on is an inside job. My role is to stay energized and to encourage others to do the same. Living lights on creates a vibrational ripple effect that benefits us all. So, my primary job is to hold my energy. From there, I then can lead effectively as a business owner, relationship partner, parent, etc.

Q. What changes are others noticing about you?

Gary One critical aspect of my relationship with Cathy is based on the fact that I am responsible for my own energy. In our marriage, my number one job is to be conscious of my own energy and do what lights me up and to create space for Cathy to do likewise. We give more to each other when we are vibrant. I have brought this same concept when working with my clients who are business leaders. There is real power when everyone in an organization is responsible for their own energy and creates space for their co-workers to be responsible for theirs as well. Can you imagine the possibilities if organizations adopted this lights on leadership approach? This way of leading is the subject of our next book.

Cathy Practicing Clarity has changed my neural pathways so I don't even consider some lights off options anymore. For example, I used to get panic attacks. Now, I have trained myself to be conscious of the anxious feeling and then immediately shift my focus to lights on thinking. When I first told Gary about my anxiety, he was concerned because he had not dealt well with other's anxious behaviors in past relationships. Gary comments. In our five years together, I have seen Cathy become anxious only once, briefly. She immediately shifted out of it into more effective behavior. Science has proven it, spiritual people have known it, and now I live with someone who has transformed at the cellular level.

Q. What has been the most challenging part of your path?

Gary Twenty-five years ago, I went broke in a business. I suffered for ten years before emotionally beginning to deal with it at a retreat called The New Warrior Weekend. That weekend was the beginning of my spiritual journey. Over the years I have used what I learned from my mistakes to help other CEOs and business owners. Ironically, my failures supported me in becoming a more effective coach and consultant. Recognizing this has been both a challenge and a blessing for me.

Cathy It was learning how to hold my own energy and teach others to maintain theirs also—without apology or compromise. Doing this involved leaving a twenty-eight-year marriage and running my company alone. As director of Clarity, I learned to focus on doing what I'm good at and let others do the rest. I learned to delegate well and hire the right people.

Q. What is your earliest memory? Why do you remember it?

Gary Reading a book to my mother for the first time when I was four. I don't know if this is an actual memory or has become one through family stories. But I can certainly see it clearly.

Cathy I have a very vivid childhood memory because I almost drowned. I was two years old, walking with my dad on a bridge over an ice-covered pond. I was fascinated by the ice and just jumped off the bridge and fell through the ice. I have a distinct memory of feeling pressure on my chest and holding my breath. My dad pulled me out and gave me CPR.

Q. Who are your mentors? What have you learned from them?

Gary My male friend who invited me to the New Warrior Weekend and gave me the opportunity to self-reflect in a supportive atmosphere. A former girlfriend who brought me to the Pacific Church of Religious Science. The church's minister, Dr. Kathy Hearn, and another woman, Suzette Wehunt, who served as my Science of Mind practitioner. Cathy Hawk, my wife, who is my greatest teacher.

Cathy Sustainable gardening practices because they taught me about energy. I learned to detect aliveness and watch it move through systems. I also discovered the concept of right plant, wrong place and used it to help clients find careers and relationships to cultivate their perennial aliveness. Other mentors include: 1) my son who was an honor to raise, 2) Michael and Justine Toms of NPR's *New Dimensions*, who are friends of the heart, 3) Dr. Ranaan Rauch, a chi gong master who taught me the golden treasures, and authors Deepak Chopra and Caroline Myss, who continued my energy education. I also acknowledge the early EST-based courses such as Mindspring (now PSI) and Landmark because they built the foundation on which we all stand. My greatest mentor is my husband, Gary Hawk, who supports me energetically so we radiate out to the world.

Q. What is the greatest challenge facing society?

Gary Helping people see we are all one—all part of the same massive energy ball. If we had gotten this concept, we wouldn't have had 9/11 or Desert Storm. My friend, a Jehovah's Witness, commented that he and I agree seventy percent of the time; it's the other thirty percent that causes war. Conflict can be avoided by setting the intent to be fully present, see others at the level of their spirit, and be connected from that space. Cathy's cell phone has a logon message that says, "My intention is . . ." This helps her set the right intention for every call.

Cathy Getting people over their inertia, the unconscious pattern of accepting that this is the way it is. We have forty people in our database who are motivated enough to talk with us but won't commit to taking our course. We recently had a woman come who waited nine years before signing up to come to a retreat. Afterwards she said, "This has been such an important weekend for me. I should have called sooner."

Q. What advice would you give someone just starting his or her spiritual path?

Gary Give yourself permission to lead a fully vibrant life in which you receive all you desire. Most of us don't go there because we feel unworthy or are scared to look inside. I had a business owner say, "Can I still do Clarity if I don't like self-reflection?" I replied, "Of course. We're not asking you to revisit old wounds. We're encouraging you to step back from your life and decide whether what you're doing energizes or drains you. Spend time focusing on what lights you up." Successful people have one thing in common—a passion for what they do. Our workshops are all about the "what," finding what energizes you. We don't even talk about how to make it happen until the last day.

Cathy Stop doing anything that doesn't rate a 7.5 or higher (out of 10) on your personal satisfaction scale. When you follow your calling, you will attract more of what you want in life. Knowing what you want allows the universe to take over the how. This is the Law of Attraction at its finest. You then will start asking journalistic questions such as, "What do I need to know for this next step?" rather than strategy questions such as, "How will I accomplish all these tasks?" Defining the what before the how helps you live lights on.

Q. What are your practices for connecting to your higher purpose?

Gary I pray to the God of Clarity. Everything I need is in this spiritual path. It builds on what I learned in Religious Science and makes sense to me intellectually, emotionally, and spiritually. Cathy and I also take care of our physical health by exercising every day.

Cathy We live who we are. We surround ourselves with beauty, keep our thoughts and actions in integrity, and maintain balance in our environment. In our home, we use eco-friendly products, cultivate a Xeriscape garden, and have good feng shui, or harmonious energy flow. When our clients come for a visit, they always thank us for walking our talk. I am more ritualistic than Gary in my practices. For example, I spend time in my garden and do my daily rituals. In the past, I used to walk a labyrinth every day as meditation.

Q. How do you use these practices when you get out of balance?

Gary When I'm busy, I sometimes get lost in left-brain activities. That's when I use Clarity's tools to bring me back into focus on my energy and my vision. Cathy and I do use a check-in process together every day. This keeps us grounded, connected, grateful, and intentional every day.

Cathy Gary and I practice our team meeting approach, checking in with each other to make sure we're aligned and not going to scatter. We enjoy our work so much that we do get busy and the day slips by before we've planned dinner. Fortunately, Whole Foods is around the corner.

Q. How do you balance planning with remaining open to opportunity?

Gary I am more left brained, so when I get stuck in analysis, I use Clarity's tools to remember my vision and what energizes me. Those things get me back on track.

Cathy I start the day by asking for guidance and remain open to it throughout the day. Clarity is an easy vehicle to ride in because it lights up both my right and left brain. As Daniel Pink writes in his book, *A Whole New Mind*, we need both an MBA and an MFA.

Q. If you received $100,000, how would you spend it?

Gary I would invest the money in Clarity's marketing and product development so the work could reach even more people. Then, I would ask Cathy for her $100,000 to double our efforts. If you gave me $1 million, I would buy a Porsche.

Cathy The money wouldn't change Clarity's purpose or direction. It simply would accelerate everything we are doing. For example, we would hire a full-time manager for our production company to complete our books, river maps, and web-based learning program. With the money, we could make more exquisite choices, such as having a fold-out color map in our second book, *Lights on Leadership*.

Q. If you had thirty seconds with someone in an elevator, what three things would you tell the person to do to be joyful, peaceful, and whole?

Gary A friend once quoted his eighty-year-old meditation instructor who said, "Joy is the present moment with nothing added." If that didn't work, I'd say, "Get a life!" "Get a life" means living in the field of all possibilities and doing what energizes and enlivens you.

Cathy I would ask the person to take a breath, get present, and decide whether he or she is energized or drained. Then, I would encourage him or her to do whatever it takes to create more energy in his or her system.

Q. What books or resources have helped you the most? Why?

Gary The best resource is relentlessly and ruthlessly holding your own energy. To do this, you also must observe your near field, the loved ones in your life. If some of them drain you, then negotiate a way to be lights on, or let them go. Like-minded friends, a faith community, an enlightening book, etc. can all support you in maintaining your energy. My best resource is my marriage to the master coach, Cathy.

Cathy My goal is to live vibrantly in every moment. It is sacred selfishness because when my lights are on, everything I touch fills with energy. When my lights are off, I drain others and myself. So the best resource is being vibrant and forming enlightened partnerships with others.

Q. What would you like to be written on your tombstone?

Gary I want my tombstone to say, "Starting Over." I jokingly said this to my son because he has seen me start over in different careers and marriages his entire life. When I die, I'm starting over spiritually and hope Cathy can catch up!

Cathy I want my ashes sprinkled over the garden and my tombstone to read, "She Died Alive." This means I lived every moment infusing others and myself with energy. My light would not disappear; it would just take a different form.

CATHY AND GARY HAWK

"To love yourself, truly love yourself, is to finally discover the essence of personal courage, self-respect, integrity, and self-esteem. These are the qualities of grace that come directly from a soul with stamina."
- Caroline Myss

"Don't believe what anyone tells you. Experience God for yourself."
Janice Hoffman, Relationship Expert and Author

Janice Hoffman is a relationship expert and author of the award winning book, *Relationship Rules: 12 Strategies for Creating a Love That Lasts*. Featured on television, radio, and in numerous articles, Janice specializes in helping men and women learn skills to improve the quality of their relationships. For nearly twelve years, Janice was a certified Mars Venus Facilitator and served as the training director for John Gray's Mars Venus Institute. Since 1998, she has been a member of the National Speakers Association and has been nominated NSA/Colorado Member of the Year three times. She also is a member of the Colorado Independent Publishers Association and the Colorado Professional Clergy Association.

Q. What experiences put you on your spiritual path?

A. My spiritual path began with Erhard Seminars Training (known as EST) in 1978 and deepened after the birth of my three children who were sick as babies. My youngest son almost died due to a birth defect and was still very ill after his first surgery. By then, I was in so much pain I knew I had to find a way out. Someone mentioned going to Unity Church of Boulder. At the church, I took the yearlong program, *A Course in Miracles*. Each week, I was asked to write a meditation based on the course material. This experience led to my teaching meditation for thirteen years and *A Course in Miracles* for seven. In September 1999, I became an ordained minister.

Q. How did these experiences change you?

A. I am aware of how fortunate I am to be living the life I have cocreated with God. I cherish each moment, experience, and friend—knowing everything can change in a heartbeat. In

2000, I was walking down the street and a guy reading tarot cards cheerily asked, "How are you doing this fine day?" to which I replied, "It's a day." He responded, smiling, "Well, aren't you lucky to be in the five percent of the world's population born in the U.S.?" That statement changed how I looked at life. Being a woman born in the U.S. and living in Colorado is pretty darn good. It doesn't take a spiritual leader to change your life. Sometimes it is just some guy on the street asking how you are.

Q. What has been the most challenging part of your path?

A. I used to blame myself when things did not work out the way I had planned. It was difficult pulling myself out of disappointment. Now, I trust God completely. This perspective challenges me to realize and affirm that God and I cocreate everything. When disappointments come my way, I can lift myself out with ease and grace.

Q. What changes are you noticing about your life and the world?

A. When I first began studying *A Course in Miracles*, I achieved a state of bliss that I hadn't been able to achieve previously. I wanted more of this feeling but didn't know how to exchange my pain for peace. Through months of practice, I experienced peace more and more, realizing that it, not pain, was becoming the norm. As this change occurred, people came into my life who were spiritually like-minded, grounded, and caring. People continue to come in and out of my life as I grow. I treasure their support and love.

Q. What changes are others noticing about you?

A. People notice that my relationship with God has become the focal point of my life. I strive to live a life of integrity. I have learned that trusting God means trusting no matter what the circumstance. It means letting go of beliefs that don't serve me. People tell me they are afraid to follow their intuition. I tell them, "Be afraid not to follow it."

RELATIONSHIP EXPERT AND AUTHOR

Had I not followed my intuition when my youngest son was born, he would have died.

Q. What is your earliest memory? Why do you remember it?
A. When I was age five, I remember knowing about God and talking to him. Over the years, I have come to the realization that, just like a parent, God does not care what or how I call upon him, he just cares that I do.

Q. Who are your mentors? What have you learned from them?
A. Best selling author and relationship expert, Dr. John Gray, whose mentoring and training shaped my career.

Bart and Maia Berens, former directors of the Mars Venus Institute, who have been role models for living a life of integrity.

Actor Ted Neeley, who played Jesus in *Jesus Christ Superstar*, from whom I learned how to be fully present with people. The night we met, Ted invited me to the show's cast party, a very exclusive event. I realized that if this good fortune could happen, then anything is possible.

Dr. John R. Lilly, the surgeon who saved my son's life. My son and I visited him every year until he passed away. In his honor, I still keep a picture of my son and him in our home. My one regret is that I did not tell Dr. Lilly I loved him. I was too afraid of what he might think. I didn't even get to say goodbye before he died. I promised myself I would not hold back ever again.

Manny Viarrial, my dance instructor, who has given me a new way of seeing and showing up in the world. By loving me unconditionally (and I him), he has taught me the power of forgiveness and inspires me to be a better person. Because of Manny, I get to live my dream every time I compete on the dance floor.

JANICE HOFFMAN

Q. What is the greatest challenge facing society?

A. We need more leaders—people asking questions and deciding for themselves what truth is. When we don't question authority, we become too willing to accept what others tell us. The media continually feeds us fear and companies often misrepresent the truth. Recently, I saw a pharmaceutical advertisement offering a booster pill to help your antidepressant work better. When I turned down the volume, the ad appeared to sell happiness. Antidepressants don't make you happy. They dull your feelings. If we don't question what is around us, we will end up with a population of overanxious, overmedicated followers unable to make healthy choices.

Q. What advice would you give someone just starting his or her spiritual path?

A. Experience God for yourself by exploring different paths. See what resonates. When you locate a spiritual home, go deeper by asking questions. The more you learn, the more questions there are. Find mentors from whom to gather information to make your own decisions. Each mentor will give you the next puzzle piece in your journey.

Q. What are your practices for connecting to your higher purpose?

A. I weave several spiritual practices into daily life. In the morning, I meditate on quotes from Neale Donald Walsch and Joel Osteen. As I go about my tasks, I ask questions such as, "Does God give and take away?" or "Is God everywhere all the time or must we invite him in?" Before giving presentations, I ask God to let my thoughts, words, and actions be his so I say and do what's in everyone's highest good. I stay connected to Spirit through visual reminders, such as quotes around the house and an alter in my room. I also talk with my loved ones, including those who have passed away. At night, I lie in bed and thank all the parts of my body for serving me well.

Q. How do you use these practices when you get out of balance?

A. When I find myself getting impatient or frustrated, I take a deep breath and remind myself of all the blessings—the things that are working—in my life. This practice infuses me with positive energy and restores my peace of mind.

Q. How do you balance planning with remaining open to opportunity?

A. Planning without attachment to outcome is my goal. I stay in balance by trusting God and flowing in universal law. Even when it is hard, I believe that unexpected, wonderful opportunities will come to pass.

Q. If you received $100,000, how would you spend it?

A. I would start a nonprofit for single parents who could come and receive vouchers to buy necessities such as groceries, medical care, etc. I would donate a portion to deaf women and children in the U.S. and other countries. In regions with scarce resources, deaf children experience even more prejudice. I would find innovative ways to bring more of my relationship coaching to the deaf community.

Q. If you had thirty seconds with someone in an elevator, what three things would you tell the person to do to be joyful, peaceful, and whole?

A. Show your appreciation for others by complimenting and thanking them. This practice not only creates beneficial chemical and hormonal changes in the brain, it also nurtures the soul. Pay forward love and support by giving without expectation. It will come back to you, most likely from an unforeseen source. Remember you don't have to be a super-hero. It is enough to be of value to just one person each day.

Q. What books or resources have helped you the most? Why?
If I were on a desert island and could take only two books, I would bring *Conversations with God: An Uncommon Dia-*

JANICE HOFFMAN

logue (Book 1), by Neale Donald Walsch and *A Course in Miracles*. I participate in the Dances of Universal Peace in Boulder, Colorado. Through dancing, I actively praise God with my whole body.

Q. What would you like to be written on your tombstone?
A. "Thank you to all who loved and helped me become who I am."

A. Anything else?
A. Be impeccable with your thoughts. Choose your words and actions carefully because you cannot take them back. Show your appreciation. You may not get another chance. As I mentioned, Dr. Lilly died before I had the chance to show my love. My goal is to live a life worth living, without regret. So far, so good.

RELATIONSHIP EXPERT AND AUTHOR

"Let go of the word 'I.'"
Sarabjeet Kaur, Sikh Religion

Sarabjeet Kaur is a homemaker. She was born in Delhi, India and later moved to California with her husband. In California, Sarabjeet was part of an elementary school multicultural program that taught students about different world religions. Sarabjeet has a master's degree in computer science from California University.

Q. What experiences put you on your spiritual path?

A. I learned about spirituality from my parents who created a home that revered God. Every morning, my mom and dad woke up early to pray and read sacred books. As I began studying the Sri Guru Granth Sahib, the Sikh Holy Scripture that embodies the wisdom of the ten Gurus, I started to feel greater peace. I realized that everything in life is a gift from God.

Q. How did these experiences change you?

A. I see the divine in everything and know that God is with me. For example, he rescues me from danger, like the time our car careened down an embankment and we were supernaturally lifted out unharmed. I honor God by being kind in heart, pure in spirit, and faithful in worship. I'm also careful not to hurt anyone. If someone harms me, I accept it as my karma. I did something in the past that is revisiting me as a lesson.

Q. What changes are you noticing about your life and the world?

A. I used to complain when bad things happened. Now, I look for God's hidden message. This inquiry requires patience as the lessons reveal themselves slowly. I draw great comfort from reading and reciting the Gurbani, the writings of the

131

ten Gurus, and practicing Japji Sahib, repetitive prayer in which I repeat God's name like a mantra.

Q. What changes are others noticing about you?

A. My parents and siblings say that even though I was the youngest child, I never acted spoiled. Now they perceive me working harder than ever. For example, I earned a master's degree in computer science while raising my two sons.

Q. What has been the most challenging part of your path?

A. I grew up in a protective atmosphere surrounded by my extended family. When I got married, I moved to the United States, where I had no relatives. Alone, I grew depressed and began pondering spiritual questions such as, "What is life? Why am I here?" I turned to the Sri Guru Granth Sahib for answers. There I found strength and peace. Now I feel very comfortable being by myself.

Q. What is your earliest memory? Why do you remember it?

A. When I was four, a neighborhood boy took money from his parents to buy cookies on his birthday. As he crossed the street, a car hit him and I saw his body lying in the road. I'll never forget his tragic death. I also remember my grandmother to whom I was very attached. She passed away a month after I gave birth to my second son. The day before she died, she asked about my son and me, but we did not get a chance to see her. She used to visit me in my dreams.

Q. Who are your mentors? What have you learned from them?

A. In India, I had very good instructors who taught both academic and life lessons. Now I teach my children through reading and telling mythological stories. I also encourage them to participate in Shabad Kirtan, the singing and playing of hymns, at our gurdwara or Sikh temple. Our souls, just like our bodies, need nourishment to grow.

Q. What is the greatest challenge facing society?

A. Our narrow-minded focus on the "I" or "ego" traps us in self-ishness, materialism, and division. We erect artificial barriers to gain power and exploit others for our own purposes. What do we hope to achieve? Nothing good can come from fear and domination. Instead, we should focus on respect, peace, and goodwill. God is oneness. From one Gem, all people and faiths were created. God would never ask us to hurt others in his name. When we do, we crush this Gem into rubble.

Q. What advice would you give someone just starting his or her spiritual path?

A. Let go off the word "I." Replace it with being good and treating others as equals. Don't get into a debate about God. There are many paths to the divine. Study all of them so you can enhance your understanding of the creator and the world. Use scientific and technological advances to grow closer to each another. These advances give us the chance to share our best spiritual teachings and practices.

Q. What are your practices for connecting to your higher purpose?

A. I have a separate room in my house for meditation and prayer. In this room, I keep my holy books, e.g., Nitnem Gutka, Sukhmani Sahib, etc., covered in silk cloth and my son's drums, tabla, for playing hymns called shabad kirtan. Every morning, I enter this sacred space with full devotion, covering my head and opening my books with great reverence, as though I am waking the Guru. I try to read the books three times a day: in the morning, evening, and at bedtime. These practices are important for keeping calm during this challenging time. According to Indian mythology, this era is called Kalyug, or the Dark Age. It is a time when greed, violence, and lust take us far from God. To remain safe, I read holy scripture, practice repetitive prayer, and worship at the gurdwara.

Q. How do you use these practices when you get out of bal-

SARABJEET KAUR

ance?

A. In addition to doing my spiritual practices, I look for ways to help others. Being of service releases my fears and brings me closer to God. Despite her infirmities, my mother is always kind and helpful to people. Her example is an inspiration to me.

Q. How do you balance planning with remaining open to opportunity?

A. As a mother and computer professional, I plan my schedule but remain flexible so I can respond to things as they arise. At night, I review my day to see where I made mistakes. If I have been unkind, I reflect on the situation, pray, and mend myself. I learned this approach from reading the Indian poet Kabir who wrote, "God is the breath of all breath."

Q. If you received $100,000, how would you spend it?

A. I would spend money on academic education, physical rehabilitation, and career training for poor people, or give the money to organizations that help the homeless and hungry.

Q. If you had thirty seconds with someone in an elevator, what three things would you tell the person to do to be joyful, peaceful, and whole?

A. I would ask the person about his or her situation. Then, I would listen with an open heart. Sometimes just having the chance to speak helps the person feel better. I also would invite the individual to close his or her eyes, feel the divine, and repeat God's name over and over again until he or she felt calm.

Q. What books or resources have helped you the most? Why?

A. Sri Guru Granth Sahib—The Sikh Holy Scripture, compiled by the ten Gurus, which draws from many faiths to describe God and the way to live. I particularly like the hymns called Sukhmani Sahib, which means "peace in your mind."

Sikh Religion

Nitnem Gutka—Small books that contain parts of the Sri Guru Granth Sahib.

Sri Dasam Granth Sahib—Poems written by Guru Gobind Singh, the tenth (and last human) Sikh Guru, who declared the Sri Guru Granth Sahib, the living embodiment of the ten Gurus.

Amirt Kirtan—The chanting of hymns containing the Gurus—and other—holy writings, accompanied by instruments.

Q. What would you like to be written on your tombstone?
A. I am going to be cremated. I want my children to remember the values I have taught so they will be kind and lead good lives. I have tried to set this example for them.

Q. Anything else?
A. I encourage people to respect and love one another. Through this practice, they will grow closer to each other and God. As my sons sing in the kirtan, "With your feet, walk in the way of the Lord. Your soul shall be forever peaceful."

SARABJEET KAUR

"True nobility . . . is about
being better than you used to be."
"Don't die with your music still inside you."
- Dr. Wayne Dyer

Reprinted from The Power of Intention (2004) and Excuses Begone! (2009)
by Dr. Wayne Dyer with permission of Hay House, Inc., Carlsbad, CA.
www.hayhouse.com.

"It's your choice to come here, to be here, to bring your joy."
Rhetah Kwan, Life Coach

Rhetah Kwan is a consummate facilitator, consultant, innovative instructor, and a unique blend of mentor, mediator, and life coach with a solid commitment to health and well-being. She has studied herbology, massage, chi kung, and nutrition in her personal quest for health. For the last thirty-five years Rhetah has consulted with allopathic and alternative providers all over the U.S. who implement electronic medical records systems. She lives in Portland, Oregon with her husband, David Kleber, an astrologer. Rhetah is a conscious life and business coach who loves to help people improve their health so they can take back their dreams and live a life of choice.

Q. What experiences put you on your spiritual path?
A. I was born on my spiritual path. As a child, I spent time alone in my mother's garden, which I thought of as my secret garden. This alone time was very powerful because I would dialogue internally with all kinds of beings in nature. I remember feeling called to nature and being grateful for my time there.

Q. How did these experiences change you?
A. I have an all-knowing eye, a holding place that observes and stores experiences. Later, when I am alone, I review these experiences and see their lessons for the others involved and me. I learn on multiple levels, which helps me work with the experiences more deeply.

Q. What has been the most challenging part of your path?
A. The most challenging part was growing up in a family not on a spiritual path. My calling to leave the family was so great

that I would sleepwalk at night. I often woke up in the middle of the field in back of my house and would wait until it became light to return home. I was too scared to walk in the dark. While I didn't remember sleepwalking, I would remember the visions I received. When I finally left home to live with a family friend, I dreamt that half her daughter's body was being eaten by cancer. In the dream, her daughter was calling to me and I couldn't find her. I woke up pounding on the neighbor's door and when they answered, I was so scared that I ran, tripped, and broke my ankle. The daughter died later that year, on my birthday. No one knew she was sick, as I had not told anybody about my dream.

Q. What changes are you noticing about your life and the world?

A. Life becomes easier and lighter as I follow my passion and do what brings me joy. When I live my joy, I am able to get out of the way and be of greater service. I'm a people opener. I connect people to their inner genius, that part of themselves that knows exactly who they are and where they want to go. The world has become a softer, gentler, safer place because of this connection. I know I'm going to be shown the changes I need to make so that they will happen with grace. I also know we are very young as a culture, like a baby horse trying to walk after being born. We stumble, fall, and learn something each time we get back up.

> "We cannot take the spirit out of anything we do."

Q. What changes are others noticing about you?

A. When people befriend me, they treat me like a family member right away. They feel I'm always going to be there for them. What has been harder is to evolve relationships and, in time, to someday let them go. People are not always happy when it is time to move on but I am comfortable doing so because I know it fosters growth and serves our highest good.

LIFE COACH

Q. What is your earliest memory? Why do you remember it?

A. My earliest memory is wondering why I was born into my family. I had difficulty bonding because I felt so different. I was closest to my Russian grandmother who raised me when I was very young, even though she spoke no English and was paralyzed on one side. I often pondered how I came to be in my family while sitting in my magic garden.

> "We all have a divining rod within that lets us know our purpose."

Q. Who are your mentors? What have you learned from them?

A. I have had a lot of mentors, partially because I believe there are many paths to Spirit. The artists in Laguna Beach taught me about life as I watched them paint. I also learned from hearing Timothy Leary lectures at Mystic Arts and various speakers at the Hare Krishna Temple. My husband David has taught me more than anyone and Taylor Hartman, a brilliant behavioral psychologist who rekindled my purpose in the world, has also been a mentor.

I love to sing and was trained by an opera coach with whom I had deep philosophical discussions. Although I was one of his best students, I knew I would not make it as an opera singer because I was not willing to sell myself by dressing up and having tea with wealthy patrons. I continued to sing in church choirs but eventually would get kicked out because I never showed up on Sundays. I have pictures of Gandhi, Mother Teresa, and the Hindu God Ganesha that reflect my drawing from different faith traditions. Ganesha and Taoism particularly resonate with me.

Q. What is the greatest challenge facing society?

A. People need to get in touch with themselves, with their core, so that what they do matches who they are. I like to ask,

RHETAH KWAN

"What would you be doing right now if you were helping yourself?" People answer from their core, a place of love and clean motive. When we work from this place, anything is possible. When we work in the reverse direction, from the outside in, we do not get the result we want—no matter how good the cause. It's like laws we put in place to get people to do the right thing. They don't work because they are externally imposed. When we come from love, we do not need laws because we are aligned with our purpose.

> **"I like my schedule to breathe."**

Q. What advice would you give someone just starting his or her spiritual path?

A. We all have a divining rod within that lets us know our purpose. People should ask, "What brings me joy? How can I work outward from this place?" Then, they should keep checking in to make sure they are coming from love, from clean motive, forgiving anything that does not come from this place.

Q. What are your practices for connecting to your higher purpose?

A. To be alive is to be connected to my higher purpose. We cannot take the spirit out of anything we do. To enhance this connection, I like to sing. When I sing, the world is healed. When I forget to sing, I know something is wrong. Also, when I am in water, I let go completely and just exist. The truth is always with us but when things grow really quiet, it gets amplified.

Q. How do you use these practices when you get out of balance?

A. When I get off track, I connect with my husband. He reminds me to let go and live in the present. He also gives me perspective when I am upset with someone, asking "Does that remind you of anyone you know?" This question helps me see the situation as an opportunity to learn. I am responsible for everything I experience. I also like to turn on music and sing. I particularly like *Essence*, by Diva Premal.

Q. How do you balance planning with remaining open to opportunity?

A. Planning is a structure to climb on that frees me to be in the moment. I'm aware how my different commitments fit together, so I can accommodate them and leave breathing room in between. I like my schedule to breathe. When something important comes up, I honor the change by making appropriate arrangements. Overall, I feel guided in my scheduling, so I experience this balance as organic and smooth.

Q. If you received $100,000, how would you spend it?

A. I would sit down with my husband and a few other planet watchers and seek their advice on how to distribute the funds. Most likely I would give a large portion to environmental causes.

Q. If you had thirty seconds with someone in an elevator, what three things would you tell the person to do to be joyful, peaceful, and whole?

A. Find your joy. Make health the center of your life. From this center, surround yourself with people who love you. As Taylor Hartman says, "Get yourself, get out of the way, and get others."

Q. What books or resources have helped you the most? Why?

A. If people did the three things I just mentioned and read these books, they would be well on their path.

Zero Limits: The Secret Hawaiian System for Wealth, Health, Peace, and More, by Joe Vitale and Ihaleakala Hew, Ph.D

> **"One cannot consent to creep when one feels the impulse to soar."**
> **- Helen Keller**

RHETAH KWAN

The Diamond Cutter: The Buddha on Strategies for Managing Your Business and Your Life, by Geshe Michael Roach
The Lazy Man's Guide to Enlightenment, by Thaddeus Golas
The Color Code and *Playing Life To Win,* by Dr. Taylor Hartman
Autobiography of a Yogi, by Paramahansa Yogananda
The Spontaneous Healing of Belief: Shattering the Paradigm of False Limits, by Gregg Braden
Initiation, by Elisabeth Haich
The Metabolic Plan: Stay Younger Longer, by Stephen Cherniske, M.S.

Q. What would you like to be written on your tombstone?
A. If I had a tombstone, it would say, "It's your choice." Most likely, I will be cremated and have my ashes—my molecules—scattered in a place that brings people the most joy.

Q. Anything else?
A. A quote by Helen Keller, "One cannot consent to creep when one feels the impulse to soar."

"The body in an expression of divinity."
Marguerite McCormack, Licensed Professional Counselor

Marguerite McCormack is a consultant, trainer, and practitioner in the field of trauma. She works nationally with issues of trauma, disaster, organizational trauma dynamics, and vicarious trauma. She is the former Director of Trauma Practice at Jefferson Center for Mental Health, the former project director of Columbine Connections, the community-based response to the shootings at Columbine High School, and the former coordinator of the Student Counseling Center at the University of Colorado at Denver. She is one of the principal authors of the *Colorado State Mental Health Curriculum for Intervention in Disasters*, *Introduction to Trauma Therapy*, and *Working with Children in Disasters*, and *Vicarious Traumatization and Burnout in First Responders*.

Q. What experiences put you on your spiritual path?

A. I was raised in a Catholic family among women of great spiritual stamina. When I began questioning the Church in my teens, I discovered *Zen and the Art of Motorcycle Maintenance*, by Robert Pirsig, and it set off a bomb in my life. I began reading Alan Watts' books, studying Buddhism and other faiths, and meditating at a zendo.

Q. How did these experiences change you?

A. Catholicism's aestheticism awakened me to beauty. However, the faith's demeaning view of women led me to question authority and seek a new path. When I heard the Buddhist concept, "life is suffering," I wanted release through practicing non-attachment. Buddhism and *A Course in Miracles* helped me realize that most of what I experience is an illusion. This awareness influenced my choice to become a therapist, a choice no one, even I, could have predicted given my rebellious past.

Q. What has been the most challenging part of your path?

A. Early on, the most challenging parts were leaving Catholicism in my late teens and caring for an ailing son as a young mother. When I left Catholicism, I was angry and self-destructive. When my son was ill, I questioned what kind of God could hurt small children. Now, the most challenging part is accepting that, despite my seeking and education, I know only a scintilla of what really is. The distortion that happens as divine energy travels down through the world makes it impossible to know more.

Q. What changes are you noticing about your life and the world?

A. I am not even certain that I'm here right now. This is disquieting because I have been invested in the delusion of reality, the delusion that I am separate from God and others. My separation, and the irresponsible thoughts and actions that arose from it, have caused suffering. I now see my role as being similar to that of the psychologist in Jim Harrison's novel *Dalva*. People can tear themselves apart in all the myriad of ways available to them, and it is my job to help them stop. People are suffering from the idea of separation and it is my job to help them see past this delusion. But they must be willing to see. It's like the old joke, "How many therapists does it take to change a light bulb? Only one, but the light bulb has to want to change."

Q. What changes are others noticing about you?

A. I'm going through a period of retreat, what Buddhists call being "in the Bardo." So I'm not as available to others. In this quiet period, I'm beginning to see how to better support people's spiritual evolution and make their livelihoods more sustainable. For example, I work with clergy and the structure of their positions is frequently untenable. They are asked to be the chief executive officer, doctor, counselor, and public relations director of their parish. This approach is inimical to their spiritual and physical health.

Q. What is your earliest memory? Why do you remember it?

A. At age two and a half, my cousin Patty Ann and I were running through long, dewy grass in the early morning near a weeping willow tree. Afterwards, we went into the house and put our wet feet into the dryer to warm them. I remember this experience because of its sheer sensate pleasure and delight.

Q. Who are your mentors? What have you learned from them?

A. My third grade teacher, Sister Antonia, whose relationship with God was like a friendly wrestling match. I appreciated her humor, sassiness, and zest for life, despite her advanced age and diabetes. Other spiritual mentors include: Ammachi, St. Teresa of Avila, Hildegard of Bingen, Pema Chödrön, St. John of the Cross, Andrew Harvey, Carl Jung, the Dalai Lama, C. S. Lewis, Reinhold Niebuhr, Rainer Maria Rilke, and Rumi. Catholicism led me to perceive the body—and women as an extension of the body—as sinful. My mentors showed me that the body is an expression of divinity. When I pay attention to how my body feels, I am led to God. When I pay attention to what my mind says, it's a crapshoot. A strong intellect can remove spiritual barriers but it cannot get us to God.

Q. What is the greatest challenge facing society?

A. We're killing the planet. What's happening to the planet is analogous to what's happening to women. Gaia—the Earth and women—give and give and give until they can give no more. If we fail to recognize and reward their contribution, then our time here is limited. As Kathleen Norris writes in *Acedia & Me*, we must adopt the perspective of future generations, confront our destructive ways, and unleash our boundless creativity for solutions.

Q. What advice would you give someone just starting his or her spiritual path?

MARGUERITE MCCORMACK

Licensed Professional Counselor

A. I would speak to the concept of God, truth, and community—what Buddhists call Buddha, Dhamma, and Sangha. I would ask what metaphor helps the person realize God. Then, I'd encourage the person to seek out a spiritual director and community that honors his or her experience of God and challenges him or her to appreciate other metaphors. Community is so important because it supports a person going through a "dark night of the soul" and reemerging into greater awareness.

Q. What are your practices for connecting to your higher purpose?

A. The most profound spiritual practice has been being a mother. My two sons have taught me patience, endurance, and humor. They mirror back to me who I am and this helps me see that it's not about me; it never has been. Also, I wake up in the morning and do spiritual reading. This week's is about turning it over to God. More and more, I realize the power of allowing God to work through me without trying to do everything myself.

Q. How do you use these practices when you get out of balance?

A. As the Dalai Lama says, "My religion is kindness." Kindness and enlightenment involve climbing back on the edge after we have fallen off. For example, yesterday, my younger son and I were criticizing each another and I was challenged not to react in anger. I stepped away, collected my heart and mind, and returned to apologize, asking, "What's really going on here?" We must return over and over again to kindness.

Q. How do you balance planning with remaining open to opportunity?

A. There's a story of the man who waited by the Ganges River for the God Shiva. When Shiva finally came, the man barked, "Go away, I'm waiting for Shiva." This story reflects our addiction to busy-ness, and God doesn't necessarily show up when we are busy. I assist my clients in performing schedule surgery, making sure they create space to nurture themselves. In my own schedule, I block off personal time, take a day to rest, and leave gaps.

Q. If you received $100,000, how would you spend it?
A. I'd spend $10,000 on a vacation to Greece and the Holy Land to rest, rejuvenate, and see with new eyes. I'd donate some to the Sisters of Charity of Leavenworth, who do wonderful work with children and trauma at the Mount Saint Vincent Home. I'd also give some to put the arts back in schools. Art is a vehicle for apprehending God. Finally, I'd put some aside for a rainy day.

Q. If you had thirty seconds with someone in an elevator, what three things would you tell the person to do to be joyful, peaceful, and whole?
A. Have a passion, get enough sleep, and love somebody or something.

Q. What books or resources have helped you the most? Why?
A. The authors I mentioned as mentors. Find your tribe—people who share your metaphor. My tribe consists of my acupuncturist, my old housekeeper, and author Robertson Davies, all of whose books I've read. When I approached Davies at a book signing, he said, "What do we have here?" Though nearly blind, I hope he recognized me as part of his tribe. He lives on through his writing.

Sometimes there are few records of great consciousnesses. Recently, Gandhi's grandson got to hear his grandfather's voice because he was open to speaking with a stranger who had known Gandhi and kept a recording of him. I once heard Yogi Bhajan say that Ram Das, the saint from the 1500s, was his spiritual teacher. Bhajan explained that great consciousnesses create a groove in the universe that you can tune into,

MARGUERITE McCORMACK

like a radio station, to help you get closer to God.

Q. What would you like to be written on your tombstone?
A. I'm going to be cremated and have my ashes scattered in the great redwood forest in Eureka, California. This forest is a church of thousand-year-old trees coexisting as one organism with one shared root system. Tibetan Buddhists believe that spirits take refuge in trees between lifetimes. So, like Saint Francis, I greet the trees saying, "Hello sister." Two places to find God are in nature and loved ones.

Q. Anything else?
A. Take care of yourself with regular habits such as good food, sleep, and exercise. If you don't take care of yourself, you may miss when God is speaking to you. For example, we lost poet Dylan Thomas too young due to self-annihilation. Contrast this with Robertson Davies, who kept writing and writing so we got to see his consciousness and contribution expand over his lifetime.

"You are the source of spiritual power in your life."
Greg Mooers, Creator of the Heart Virtue
program at Bridge2Bliss

Greg Mooers, partner at Bridge2Bliss, has developed a technique that accelerates spiritual and psychological evolution and revolutionizes the science of counseling using quantum physics principles. He has used this technique to train entrepreneurs, psychologists, ministers, Olympic Gold Medalists, and Academy and Emmy Award winning celebrities.

Greg spent more than 15,000 hours in silent meditation during his eight years as a monk. During that time, he also studied the most inspiring contributors throughout history and how they were able to motivate others, people like Mother Teresa, who was motivated by Compassion, Martin Luther King, who was motivated by Brotherhood, and Gandhi, who was motivated by Peaceful Liberation. What is it for you? Is it Loyalty, Honesty, or Freedom? Greg's three-step program will reveal what is motivating you and show you how to use quantum physics principles to create a rewarding career and fulfilling relationships.

Q. What experiences put you on your spiritual path?
A. My path started when I was four years old and had a bad flu. My temperature was up around 105 degrees and I was hallucinating. The room was closing in on me and I felt terrified. My mother, who was involved in metaphysics, was a very nurturing woman. She put a cold towel on my head and left me to rest on my bed. Somehow the cold spread throughout my entire body and I ended up freezing and having nightmares. My mother came back in and I was sitting up on the bed with my legs crossed. She tried to lay me down and my legs went straight up in the air because I was so cold and rigid. She was talking to me and I could hear her, but I couldn't

respond. So she started whispering in my ear, "Greg, just say to yourself, 'I dwell in Christ Consciousness.'" I had no idea what these words meant, but as I said them, I felt my body warm up and thaw out. The faces and images I had been seeing disappeared. After this experience, I never felt that level of fear again.

Years later, I ended up going to Sunday school and they were talking about Christ on the cross. I thought, *Oh yeah, Christ, my buddy*. I grew up in New Jersey in a tough neighborhood. Kids would bully me and I would use my affirmation, "I dwell in Christ Consciousness." Every time I used it, I felt protected and at peace. I got confirmation that I have a very personal, very close relationship with Christ. But my spiritual path is nonexclusive. I don't believe one way is better than another. I was a monk for eight years with Self-Realization Fellowship because my yearning to explore that part of myself became uncontrollable. I was so curious about what was possible. I spent many years meditating, praying, and getting to know some of the beautiful entities that had guided me earlier in life.

Q. How did these experiences change you?

A. As I mentioned, I lost my sense of fear through the flu experience. Then, when I was eighteen, I started meditating using Self-Realization Fellowship techniques. What I appreciate about Self-Realization Fellowship is that it is the "church of all religions." They believe that Hinduism, Buddhism, Christianity, and Islam all lead to the same place. There is one God and God is able to take many forms to fulfill the longings of the devotee. Paramahansa Yogananda came from India to teach us and I loved how he showed the parallels between the Hindu Bible—the Bhagavad Gita—and the Christian Bible. They both say the same things about how to conduct ourselves and develop our character. Through study and meditation, I adopted a sense of peace that I had never experienced before—the peace that comes from stillness.

During the years I was a monk, I became impassioned through studying the lives of saints and heroes. And I came up with a three-step path for how a human being can become a hero. Now I'm in a place where I could die tomorrow and my whole life would have been fulfilled. I can't believe I get to do what I do. I get to work with people who are frustrated and know there must be more to life. I tell these people, "I can work with you. You're ready. Let's get you being incredibly heroic and a humanitarian contributor."

Q. What changes are you noticing about your life and the world?
A. We all have an identity that we turn to for security. When I had an identity that I was holding onto, what I found was that life couldn't happen. Life is not a defined thing, it's a dynamic thing. I was constantly hitting walls because life was asking me to be a friend or husband and I was saying, "No, I'm an engineer. I'm a monk." So I got wrapped up in those identities. When I walked into a room, I wanted to be acknowledged for my identity.

I think what has really changed is that now I can be present. I can walk into a room passionate and curious about what wants to happen and see who I can be to make the greatest contribution. My favorite quote is, "Be the change you wish to see in the room."—a takeoff on Gandhi's famous quote. It's about being willing to adopt whatever heroic position is inviting me and holding people to a high level of account. It takes a lot of courage to do that, and yet that courage makes it a lot safer than holding onto my identity.

I originally adopted my identity to give me meaning but it was also killing me because I was holding too much structure. What does Spirit mean? There was a monk at the monastery who followed the rules to a tee. One of the other monks commented, "He follows the rules so strictly that he has lost the spirit of them. So, there is a "spirit," an essence, that's not structure.

GREG MOOERS

Q. What changes are others noticing about you?

A. The number one thing I get lately is that I am so happy and at peace. I used to be pretty difficult to be around because I always challenged beliefs. When you are eighteen years old, you know everything and nobody wants to be around you. When you are twenty-five, you're like, "Maybe there are a couple of things I could learn about life." When you are thirty-five, you're like, "I have a lot to learn." When you are fifty, you're like, "I don't know anything," so you are finally open to listening and are delightful to be around.

So, when I was eighteen, I knew a lot. I remember opening Yogananda's book *The Sayings of Paramahansa Yogananda* thinking, *I'm going to tear this to pieces. It's just another doctrine.* Instead I thought, *You know what, this is truth. This is the way it really is.* That was the first day I was actually curious instead of being a know-it-all. Einstein said, "I don't have special talents, I'm just passionately curious." That was his great skill. So, I'm a big fan of listening, of being interested, of being passionately curious instead of knowing, having answers, and telling people how to live their lives. I'm far more interested in asking people, "How do you want to live your life?" and giving them permission to explore that. The thing that has changed the most is that I've gone from being a rigid know-it-all to being someone who is genuinely curious about lots of stuff, especially people and their passions.

Q. What has been the most challenging part of your path?

A. During the years I was a monk, there was this agreement that people were materialistic and egotistical and that we should transcend this physical stuff through meditation. It was almost like I was meditating to get out of my body. The attitude of the monks was, "My body is a donkey. I will ignore it and the five senses." There is much to be said for monastic discipline, especially sexual discipline. We monks were celibate and I found tremendous power and focus in controlling those energies. But the difficult part was denying my physical existence. We're a spiritual being, but we're in a physical body. My background is engineering and quantum physics so I'm looking at this from the perspective of "What's the intention here?" My soul took a body. I have something physical to do.

When I was a monk, I was living for the day I died. I wasn't living for the day I had. One day I did a meditation and got clarity that the day I die, I'm going to wake up and say, "Thank God it was just a life!" I'm so clear there is nothing to do up there while I'm down here. People are suffering. They aren't treating each other very well because they don't know what life is really all about and what it can be.

So my challenge is being drawn to the spiritual arena and meditation, and yet knowing that I have physical things to do. The goal is to become a master of being able to keep my mind in the clouds and my feet firmly on the ground while using my hands to do really good work in the world. Otherwise, I am not cooperating with my soul's intention.

Q. What is your earliest memory? Why do you remember it?
A. When I was eighteen months old, I lived in Minneapolis, near a lake. There were stables in the backyard that housed a horse named Pedro. He had a star on his forehead. Whenever I had an opportunity, I would crawl out the back door and go sit under the horse. I loved sitting underneath him. The neighbors would be so alarmed, but my mother would calmly go out, pick me up, and bring me back into the house.

When I went through Diana Lees' equine therapy and empowerment program, I learned that horses have a heart the size of a watermelon and a brain the size of a walnut. They're all heart and they don't get their thinking in the way because their brain is so small. You show up around a horse and they are going to respond to you authentically. When I heard this

GREG MOOERS

I thought, *That's why I loved sitting underneath that horse. It was all heart.* I think the soul of the body lives in the heart. Who we know we are is the soul. If I ask you to point to yourself, what would you do? You'd point to your chest. The heart is our secret dwelling place.

Q. Who are your mentors? What have you learned from them?

A. Yogananda. Many of the monks, especially Ananda Moy. Fred Segal has been an incredible friend. A lot of my mentors have tough personalities because I'm a pretty stubborn guy. They have been able to break through that. Another mentor is Kathy Smith. She's a fitness expert who has helped me produce my workshops. She's a brilliant mentor because she doesn't take the role as being above. Instead, she's just a really good friend. Bob Heiman, founder of Epicuren Skincare, who has developed a process called SAIOE. Those are a few of the people who have had the most impact.

Q. What is the greatest challenge facing society?

A. We went through the agricultural revolution a few hundred years ago. Then we went through the industrial and information ages. Right now, we are entering the humanitarian age. If you listen to people's conversations, they are talking about what's meaningful, not about their fancy cars or new shoes. So the greatest challenge facing us is admitting that we care and shifting from an outside-in (who I am is what I own) to an inside-out (who I am is how I live my values) paradigm. It's almost as if our collective consciousness has realized that the old way is a dead-end street.

Martin Luther King was committed to brotherhood and said, "I have a dream." Gandhi was committed to peaceful liberation and said, "Be the change you wish to see in the world." We make statues to these people whereas a few hundred years ago, we would have chopped their heads off or burned them at the stake. People are honoring these heroes because we have created a culture where if you take a stand to feed twenty thousand hungry children, people will get behind you. You will get grants and invisible forces will open the door and push your efforts forward.

The funny thing is that so few people are taking this stand. But we are getting there. People are saying, "Yes, I want to make a huge contribution to humanity." When I speak to audiences, I ask, "How many of you are here today because you know you have a big contribution to make and are ready to start?" Almost every hand goes up. So I think the challenge is shifting from living outside-in to living inside-out. Once people get it, it will become so seductively compelling that they will do nothing else.

Q. What advice would you give someone just starting his or her spiritual path?

A. Kill the Buddha. Every scripture tells us that God—the kingdom of heaven—is within. We are God. If you own this power, then "greater things than this shall ye do." I've always said, "If these aren't God's hands, then God doesn't have hands." I don't see any invisible hands coming down from the clouds and cleaning things up. If people aren't going to take responsibility for humanity, then there is no God. So if you come across anything that you make greater than yourself, kill it. That's what "Kill the Buddha" means.

You are the source of spiritual power in your life. If you are giving power to something outside you, then that is the outside-in model. We are finally willing to own that this is an inside-out game. Look at Gandhi. He liberated his nation from one of the most powerful empires on the planet. He didn't do it by using some reasonable method of force. He had no army. What he had was spiritual power—the virtue of peaceful liberation that he was relentlessly willing to stand by. It was as if invisible forces were assisting him.

So don't start out praising something. Start out believing in

GREG MOOERS

yourself. Humility and surrender are the qualities monastics praise more than any other. People used to think that humility meant humbling ourselves by pretending to be small. True humility comes from taking on a project so huge that inside it, we are nothing. My commitment is that six billion people know their heart virtues. That's impossible, but I'm staying committed to that—and that's true humility.

I tell people all the time, if you are arrogant, be openly arrogant and you're safe. People will scrub you down and you're arrogance will turn into a really beautiful contribution to humanity. But if you are arrogant inside and pretend to be humble outside, that's a dangerous place to be. Ego shows up. Just keep staying bold. Bite off more than you can chew and chew it. If it doesn't kill you, you will learn something.

Q. What are your practices for connecting to your higher purpose?

A. My favorite is to just watch my breath and get present in my body. For example, right now, put your awareness in your left foot, then your right knee, then your left hip, and finally your heart. Once I am there, I realize that life is not a result. It's an experience. So what if I designed my day to have great experiences instead of just to get great results? I stay present by constantly looking at the experience of life and managing that experience, making efforts so the experience this hour is more rewarding than the last.

The only purpose for results is to give us resources to have experiences. Everything we achieve, we do to create an experience. So, the way I stay present is to stay in the experience, to be curious and say, "How can this experience be more fulfilling for everyone in the room?" Also, I meditate every morning for at least an hour. I don't know how people live without it. It's an island that I can always return to when things start sinking.

Q. How do you use these practices when you get out of balance?

A. My team has a saying: Everything is included. So anger comes up. The question is, "Would you be angry if you weren't committed to something?" The answer is, "No." If you weren't committed, you'd be apathetic. The fact that you're angry means you're committed to something beautiful. And the reason you are angry is that something is blocking it. Most people focus on the block. When I studied the lives of heroes, they didn't do that. Gandhi didn't care what the British government did. What he focused on was his commitment. So whenever someone is angry, especially in the rehab center, I just look at them and say, "Wow, what are you committed to?"

Every emotion has two aspects: the survivor aspect, which protects you, and the heroic perspective, which reflects your commitment to something. When each of my grandparents died, I had this incredibly strong feeling in my heart. Most people thought it was sadness. But, when I analyzed what I felt, I realized it was gratitude for their lives.

Pain is inevitable but suffering is optional. Resisting pain is what leads to suffering. Pain means I'm wanting or yearning for something. That's beautiful, that leads to passion. I felt pain when my grandparents died because I cared about them. If I'd resisted their deaths as a natural part of life, I would have suffered.

I'm not fond of pain but I recognize that it's telling me something. When people say, "I know how you feel," I think, *You have no idea how I feel. You can imagine only how you would feel if you were in this situation.* I try to stay in my body and not assume that I know what's going on for people. I don't let other people's pain affect me too much because I know they have their whole process for dealing with it. This detachment makes me effective in being able to guide people

GREG MOOERS

through difficult times. If I felt their pain too keenly, it would distract me from being curious and believing in their process.

Q. How do you balance planning with remaining open to opportunity?

A. The way I plan is through generating a request. So I'm constantly asking people what's most meaningful to them. What experience do they want to create? And then I get committed to that experience. After they say, "Greg, maybe you should come in and do a class or maybe I can have a coaching session with you," then I'll say, "Great, let's schedule it." So rather than setting a goal and trying to reach it, I've found that if I get really curious about people, they'll come up with a project, they'll make a request, and I'll put something on my calendar. For me, it's the difference between being a human being and being a human doing.

I schedule the things that are going to be the most rewarding experiences. This is because even though I may be able to get you to do something, if it's not a rewarding experience for you, you'll do it badly and then go find something else to do. So why don't I just find out where you really want to go and then get behind you? I have been way more successful in life and in business by being really authentic with people about what they want to create and getting committed to that. That's my plan.

Q. If you received $100,000, how would you spend it?

A. I would do what I am doing now. What I have learned about money is that its value is in creating experiences. So I would invest $100,000 dollars in the most rewarding experience I could think of at that time. Right now, I would invest it in this new venture Bridge 2Bliss and forward the vision of having six billion people know their heart virtues. Money is also called "currency." I believe that when people collect money in accounts and don't spend it, it's like water. It sits in a swamp and gets stagnant. Money is meant to be like a

Heart Virtue / Bridge2Bliss

river current—fresh, flowing, and feeding the countryside. I would fund a place for money to flow, fulfill, and edify.

Q. If you had thirty seconds with someone in an elevator, what three things would you tell him or her to do to be joyful, peaceful, and whole?

A. The first is appreciation. I would ask the person, "What do you really appreciate in your life?" The second is curiosity. The person may say, "My life is miserable. My car broke down." I would reply, "Okay, let's see if that is really true. How could your car breaking down be a good thing? Maybe you have been driving in fear, wondering when your car is going to break down. And now you can fix it. Or, maybe you really want to buy a new car." The third is courage. "Do an act of courage right now. Pick up the phone and call the one person you know you have been avoiding. When you get off the phone, you are going to feel a whole lot better."

Whenever I deal with people who are depressed, I say, "Okay, the answer is courage." It works every time. That's why all those breakthrough exercises you see such as ropes courses and bungee jumping actually work. Human beings have to do something courageous. Once you have done something courageous you say, "Oh my gosh, I did it!"

Q. What books or resources have helped you the most? Why?

A. Google. Remember how I was talking about the agricultural age, the industrial age, and the information age? I believe the information age ended with Google. We can get anything we want now. So if you are depressed, don't google depression. Search for its opposite—whatever it is that you really want. For example, google "passionate happiness" or "How can I be more joyful in my life?" You can type in anything, even "famous quotes aardvarks" and it will come up with some quotes on aardvarks.

Q. What would you like to be written on your tombstone?

GREG MOOERS

A. I'd love to have a hundred thousand people at my funeral. I would love to see six billion people know their heart virtues. I'd like to see ten more Gandhis, ten more Martin Luther Kings, and ten more Mother Teresas on the planet because I was walking on it. The greatest compliment I have been paid is when people tell me, "You got me in touch with my hero and I love my life." If I can leave thirty of these people behind, imagine what the planet will be like.

Q. Anything else?

A. We've shifted from the Newtonian concept of the universe into a more quantum model. Physical laws are about the Observer Effect and Field Theory. Human beings are the only creatures that can actually create. The way human beings create is through observing. Einstein said, "I am passionately curious." He was using the Observer Effect and amplifying it to such a degree that atoms actually revealed themselves to him, even on how they could be killed. George Washington Carver was so passionately curious about the peanut that he discovered one hundred plus uses for it. When he was asked, "How did you do that?" he said, "If you love something enough, it will share its secrets." If we really take a look at the quantum model, we see that the point of the Observer Effect is that you and I aren't separate. If I just look at you, you change.

So I believe that we are not six billion people living in one world. We are one people living in six billion unique worlds. So be the observer and use your field to draw out another person's brilliance. The word "education" comes from the root educo, which means "to draw forth." Education is really meant to draw out our brilliance. My request to you is to be passionately curious so you can draw out the brilliance in everyone. Because how does it feel to be around a know-it-all? Not great. Now, how does it feel to be deeply interested in someone without an ulterior motive? It feels terrific. Why not give that gift to everyone?

"I see myself as a midwife of the human spirit."
Melanie Mulhall, President and Founder of Dragonheart

Melanie Mulhall is an award winning writer and editor, as well as a spiritual mentor and shaman whose shamanic lineage can be traced back to Black Elk. Melanie describes herself as a midwife of the human spirit and activator of the possible who helps people open more fully into themselves as conscious human beings. Melanie holds an MA in human development counseling. In 2003, Melanie's book, *Living The Dream—A Guidebook For Job Seekers And Career Explorers*, won a First Place EVVY Award in the Spiritual/Inspiration Category.

Q. What experiences put you on your spiritual path?
A. I think I came into this life with my understanding and memories of who I really am intact. I recall understanding the spiritual nature of things at a very early age. I also picked the right family and circumstances to provide both the challenges and support I needed to face and get past my personal obstacles and grow. The fact that my parents were, themselves, mystics and members of Spiritual Frontiers Fellowship didn't hurt. The fact that we had plenty of family dysfunction didn't hurt either.

I have felt my soul nudging me on and, when necessary, kicking my butt most of my life. But it took a convergence of events involving a raccoon, an astrologer, a vision of a soul connection, and guidance that would not let me get away with living an ordinary life that pulled me away from corporate America, into shamanism, and more fully into the work I believe I came here to do. It's an evolving process.

Q. How did these experiences change you?

A. Dropping out of corporate America and becoming a shaman transformed my life. Before this turn of events, I was a mystic who assumed I would lead an ordinary life. As things shifted, I remember thinking, *Oh boy, I thought I would get away with just a little transformation, but I can see that is not going to be the case.* My soul wanted more. As a shaman's apprentice, I had to heal myself right down to the DNA and be transformed. It was a process not unlike alchemy: *calcinatio, solutio,* and so on to *mortificatio* and, ultimately, to *coniunctio.* Astrologers would say Pluto was mucking with me. All I can say is that I was close to fifty and in the process of personal transformation. At one point, I entered a "dark night of the soul" as a part of that transformation.

> "I have felt my soul nudging me on and, when necessary, kicking my butt."

Q. What changes are you noticing about your life and the world?

A. Shamanism permeates my being. I see and move through the world recognizing that I am one with everything and everyone. For example, I don't see humans as being "higher" than other animals or plants. We are all part of the same oneness and our energy continues on after death. I cannot really agree with the notion that eating plants is in some way "higher" than eating meat. The plant people are as alive as the animal people. When I eat meat or wear fur, I honor the animal that gave me nourishment or warmth. I do the same with plants. What I see in the world is that more people are becoming sensitive to this quality of oneness and acting on their understanding of it.

Q. What changes are others noticing about you?

A. It's hard to say because new people have come into my life while others have fallen away. When my corporate col-

DRAGONHEART

leagues heard I was a shaman, a few actually said, "I always expected that of you." Their recognition surprised me because I had not realized these qualities were so visible. My best friend embraced the changes, while my siblings took a little longer. My husband adapted. I have been following this path for some years now and those who have been with me over those years see my own unfolding, much in the same way as I mentor others on their spiritual paths.

Q. What has been the most challenging part of your path?

A. During my apprenticeship, I occasionally questioned my own sanity thanks to the flood of changes I was experiencing. While driving home from Boulder one day, I received a powerful vision of having spent lifetimes with the shaman to whom I was apprenticed. Guidance like that often came at inconvenient times and I just had to embrace the messiness of the transformative process. It was harder on my husband who once asked, "When is this going to be over?" I replied, "It's not. This is who I am." As I healed, I relinquished control and allowed my destiny to unfold. Unfortunately, one reason people are drawn to the Law of Attraction is their desire to control, to manipulate the world into giving them what they want. There is so much more to it than that. It's about jumping into the river of your purpose and letting it carry you. At age sixty, I feel better than ever—with the most important things I am to do yet to come.

Q. What is your earliest memory? Why do you remember it?

A. At around five years old, I remember listening to my summer bible school minister and knowing what he was saying wasn't entirely true. I also remember wanting my parents to notice me but fearing that when they did, I would be humiliated. There was a push/pull involved with being in hu-

> "Don't seek the Buddha outside yourself. Become him."

MELANIE MULHALL

man form. Even though there were six of us in my family, I often found myself alone. During this solitary time, I connected to universal energy and the spirit world. Many kids experience this connection but are socialized out of it. I managed to avoid that. My family's Irish/Scottish mystical roots no doubt played a part in that.

Q. Who are your mentors? What have you learned from them?

A. Shamans Don Antonio Arguello and Marilyn Youngbird have been mentors. Both have taught me through their examples of living in integrity, remaining true to themselves, and making helping others a priority. My parents also showed the way. They were very much into the natural world. My parents fished, were bird watchers, and star gazed. Both had an extraordinary appreciation for the present moment and a kind of impeccability in living everyday life. My father was also a writer and my mother a flower gardener, both of which are important to me now. My graduate school advisor, M'Lou Burnett Dixon, incorporated mind-body-spirit approaches into counseling long before they were popular. And Warren Ziegler's Enspiriting process helped me embody my inner spiritual voice in all that I do.

Q. What is the greatest challenge facing society?

A. Technological advances are outpacing our spiritual development. Focusing on materialism to the detriment of Mother Earth may result in our circuits getting blown when the planet's vibration elevates. Given my views on life and death (that this life is not all there is, that there is no real death), it would not be tragic if humans didn't survive. Right now, I feel hopeful that we are up to the challenge, especial-

> "Unfortunately, one reason people are drawn to the Law of Attraction is their desire to manipulate the world into giving them what they want. It's really about jumping into the river of your purpose and letting it carry you."

DRAGONHEART

ly since so many of us, shamans included, are working with people who want to help raise consciousness and restore harmony. But the solution starts with each individual taking responsibility for his or her own evolution and then extending out from there.

Q. What advice would you give someone just starting his or her spiritual path?

A. No one is just starting. We are all spiritual pilgrims walking the same path and we've been on it a long time. As Sheldon Kopp advised, "If you meet the Buddha on the road, kill him!" That is, don't seek the Buddha outside yourself. Become him by trusting what you know and strengthening your connection to God. Many believe that pursuing spiritual growth will make life easier when, in fact, life often initially gets more difficult as repressed parts of you surface for healing. Do not do this work to make things easy or to get something. Do it to become a clear vehicle for the divine. Over time, you *do* become happier as you learn to love yourself and stop wasting energy on denying who you are. Also, do things every day to recharge: meditate, spend time in nature and with positive people, read good books, and think loving thoughts.

Q. What are your practices for connecting to your higher purpose?

A. I meditate and do things that keep me grounded and focused on the present. For example, I exercise, spend time outdoors, and do sitting mediation. I pray and I also live prayerfully by moving through the world in a way that honors my being both fully human and completely divine. Most of my prayers are prayers of gratitude and prayers that focus on seeing the best possible for others and the world. In the shamanic way, one does not pray for peace, one prays peace. There is a profound difference between those two things. I sit on an energetic counsel that works to move energy on Earth in a positive way. I also mentor and encourage people in everything I do: writing, editing, shamanic work, etc. As a midwife

MELANIE MULHALL

of the human spirit, my job is to help others step into what is possible and live their dreams consciously. And that can be done everywhere.

Q. How do you use these practices when you get out of balance?

A. I use the word harmony instead of balance. People are a complex mix of mind, body, spirit, and emotions, not sections on a pie chart. So when I am out of harmony, I check in to see what's going on. Sometimes, a world event about to happen is affecting me energetically. Other times, it might be because I have not been meditating enough. When I overwork or feel I could become ill, I slow down and take time to restore my body and soul. However, there are times when spirit wants me out of harmony to nudge me to the next step in my development. For example, I once had food poisoning and it seemed to be what was necessary for me to clear some karma and move forward.

Q. How do you balance planning with remaining open to opportunity?

A. I work a lot and am sometimes overextended. Even if there are wonderful opportunities, if there are too many of them, it can become overwhelming. When that happens, if I have my wits about me, I ask my guidance to expand time for me or help mundane tasks get done easily. This helps return me to a steady state where I can do what needs to be done and receive with gratitude.

Q. If you received $100,000, how would you spend it?

A. I would ask guidance how to best spend it. Using money in a well-intentioned but inappropriate way can do more harm than good. For example, I oppose nationalized health care because throwing money at an illness mentality will just result in more sickness. I would like to see the focus placed on wellness and holistic approaches that catch disharmonies before they become physical disease. Most likely, I would give some of the money away, as guided, and keep a little for myself. In general, I use resources wisely, treating them with gratitude and respect.

Q. If you had thirty seconds with someone in an elevator, what three things would you tell the person to do to be joyful, peaceful, and whole?

A. Return to the present moment as often as you can because joy, peace, and wholeness are found here and now. Mindfulness practices—and those can include things like meditation, exercise, being in nature—work because they pull you into the now. The more moments you spend in the now, the more aware you become of divine oneness. Most of our troubles emanate from talking trash to ourselves—all the negative self-talk and thought. Take out the trash by returning to more uplifted, positive thoughts.

Q. What books or resources have helped you the most? Why?

A. I read authors such as Deepak Chopra, Matthew Fox, David Hawkins, Rupert Sheldrake, Marianne Williamson, and Jerry and Esther Hicks. I also like the poets Jalāl ad-Dīn Rumi, Rainer Maria Rilke, and Edna St. Vincent Millay and old resources that include everything from Ralph Waldo Emerson to St. Teresa of Avila.

Reading can help us on the way, but there is no substitute for personal experience. Develop a daily practice to ground, center, and connect to God. Get creative (words, music, paint). Listen to spiritual music such as Nawang Khechog's Tibetan flute or use tools like *Journey to Wild Divine*, which is a spiritually-oriented computer game that incorporates biofeedback. All of these things raise your vibration and help keep you in harmony. Also, find a spiritual community to support you on your path. As Christians say, "Where two or more are gathered, God is there" and love expands. In fact, love is the ultimate resource. Loving yourself and others is what it's all about.

MELANIE MULHALL

Q. What would you like to be written on your tombstone?

A. No tombstone. Ideally, I would have the animals receive nourishment from my remains, as I have theirs. In some cultures,
vultures are honored for their critical role in disposing of the
flesh. More likely, I will be cremated and I hope my remains
can be given to nature where they can be used by the earth.
I don't really need to be remembered because it's not about
me; it's about midwifing others. If people read something
I've written and find it helpful, then I'll have done my part in
catalyzing their growth.

Q. Anything else?

A. I see myself as a midwife of the human spirit. I help people
unfold into more of who they are and become more comfortable in human form. Regardless of the role I play—writer,
editor, shaman, spiritual mentor, consultant—what I am really doing is midwifing the human spirit.

DRAGONHEART

"What's Next, Papa?"
Victoria Munro, Cofounder, Make-it-Fly

Since the age of nine, Victoria has made long-range planning and goal setting a part of her lifestyle. At age seventeen, she owned and managed one retail flower shop, opening another at age nineteen in Liverpool, England. After moving to America in 1970, she started and managed a variety of businesses in Denver, Colorado. From sportswear and fashionable women's clothing to maid service and web design, Victoria has a wealth of experience in the manufacturing, service, import, and retail sectors.

Q. What experiences put you on your spiritual path?

A. I was discontent with life. At age nine, I set out to own a chain of flower shops. By my early twenties, I realized this dream and there was no satisfaction in it. I felt like I was going through a midlife crisis and thought, *Life has got to mean more than this!* So I began searching.

Q. How did these experiences change you?

A. Amidst my search, I sold my business, partied, and explored Buddhism and Catholicism. Then my au pair asked me to take her to an English church. The curate was preaching about Jesus calling Peter to walk on water. When Peter began to sink, Jesus saved him. That night I prayed, *God, if you're there, I'm sinking, please save me.* Later, I went to a Billy Graham crusade and heard Jesus say, Follow me. Before I knew what was happening, my feet carried me to the front, where I received Jesus as my Lord and Savior.

When I left, I looked into the clear starry sky and thought, *The world looks different—especially in Manchester where it usually rains!* So, I stopped partying and befriended the young woman who helped me receive Jesus. She and her roommates were fun and clean living. I wanted to be like them.

Q. What has been the most challenging part of your path?

A. The most challenging part is being willing to pay the price to follow Jesus. Each moment, I choose to live for Jesus rather than myself. For example, every day I get up and read the Bible—God's love letter to me. It would be easy to skip a day and sleep in but I don't because that's not what Jesus wants. I want to hear his voice and be clean before God, free of lies and other things that would keep me from him.

Q. What changes are you noticing about your life and the world?

A. I become more excited as I get closer to spending eternity with Jesus. The challenges grow bigger and I never know what's going to happen next. I'm heartbroken that some people are missing out on the greatest possible adventure—life with Jesus.

Q. What changes are others noticing about you?

A. About a year after I started following Jesus, I was talking with my mother while ironing and burnt a hole in my dress. When I saw the damage, I said, "Oh well," and let it go. My mother remarked, "Before you did this church stuff, you would have thrown that iron across the room!" My relationships also improved as I focused more on serving others. I remember my colleagues taunting me when I quit smoking. I felt no anger or temptation, only good humor.

Q. What is your earliest memory? Why do you remember it?

A. At age three, I was standing by the kitchen sink with my little sister while our housekeeper, Mary, peeled carrots. I asked Mary for a piece of carrot and she gave me one. My little sister looked up expectantly and Mary replied, "There's nothing for the dumb ones who don't ask." I thought later, *That's wisdom. There's nothing lost in asking.*

MAKE-IT-FLY

Q. Who are your mentors? What have you learned from them?

A. Judy Leonard, the young woman who helped me accept Christ at the Billy Graham crusade. I saw in her wisdom, courage, commitment, and faithfulness to doing God's work. She taught me to love God and to put him first. Pat Lawler, the leader of a London ministry. Pat is an elegant, well-spoken woman who always challenges and supports me. For example, when I was living in Iran and my husband died suddenly, Pat flew out to stay with me. Later, I learned she spent months recovering from a disease she had contracted there. Despite personal sacrifice, she was there for me and is still my best friend.

Q. What is the greatest challenge facing society?

A. God has placed a desire in our hearts to be in relationship with him, for meaning and purpose, for an exciting, fulfilling life. Some folks settle for counterfeit substitutes—money, sports, etc.—to satisfy the desire to be part of something bigger. These substitutes create a roller coaster life, as victories come and go. Get off the roller coaster and fill your heart with God.

Q. What advice would you give someone just starting his or her spiritual path?

A. Follow Jesus one hundred percent. There is nothing more fulfilling than his companionship. Speak with him and do what he asks. There is a price to pay for following Jesus. Pay it willingly, because the rewards are greater than you can imagine. Read the Bible, God's love letter to you. God speaks to us through the Bible and shows us how to live. A passage in Romans 8:15 explains it well. "This resurrection life you received from God is not a timid, grave-tending life. It's adventurously expectant as we greet God with a childlike, 'What's next, Papa?'"

VICTORIA MUNRO

Q. What are your practices for connecting to your higher purpose?

A. I wake up and talk with God about my day. Then, I read the Bible, which I've done every morning for forty-two years. God always speaks to me through scripture. This morning it was Romans 8:15, the expectancy of "What's next, Papa?" Reading God's love letter helps me live the life he wants. I am struck by God's awesome power as he stands outside of history, holding the nations in his loving hands to work his plan.

Q. How do you use these practices when you get out of balance?

A. Staying in balance means putting God first. Yesterday, I woke up and went straight to my computer to print something for my husband Dave, rather than talking with God and reading the Bible first. Starting the day with my perspective, rather than God's, caused me to erupt in anger at Dave. When I realized what I'd done, Dave and I prayed and allowed God to reconcile us. I always ask for forgiveness when I fall down saying, "I'm sorry Papa. Please forgive me. Thank you for making me clean again."

Q. How do you balance planning with remaining open to opportunity?

A. I plan and hold that plan with an open hand to God, asking, "God, do you want me to do this project?" God will reply through a feeling or scripture. Following Jesus means I'm always living on the edge of expectancy. Sometimes, it's not comfortable but it's an exhilarating and fulfilling way to live.

Q. If you received $100,000, how would you spend it?

A. I'd rather you didn't because it would bring a whole new set of headaches. If you gave it to me, I'd tithe some of it and then ask God what to do with the rest. Money can address a lot of needs but there is never enough to fix them all. Only God's love can do that.

Make-it-Fly

Q. If you had thirty seconds with someone in an elevator, what three things would you tell the person to do to be joyful, peaceful, and whole?

A. Get to know Jesus. Do what he asks. Read the Bible, his love letter to us.

Q. What books or resources have helped you the most? Why?

A. The Bible, God's love letter to you. Immerse yourself in it. As in Jeremiah 15:16, "When your words came, I ate them; they were my joy and my heart's delight, for I bear your name, O Lord God Almighty." I also like biographies about people who followed Jesus and willingly paid the price: *The Life of J. Hudson Taylor, Founder of the China Inland Mission*, by Howard Taylor and *A Chance to Die: The Life and Legacy of Amy Carmichael*, by Elisabeth Elliot.

Q. What would you like to be written on your tombstone?

A. I don't really care what's on my tombstone. I want to live my life to the fullest now, being the person God destined me to be. I want to be faithful, following God one hundred percent.

Q. Anything else?

A. Living with God is a wild ride. Do it with all your heart. You'll never be bored.

VICTORIA MUNRO

"Love Is The Movement."

\- Switchfoot

"Changing our inner reality changes our outer world."
Penney Peirce, Intuitive, Author, and Speaker

Penney Peirce is a respected and gifted intuitive empath with deep psychological understanding, visionary ability, and business sense. She is one of the early pioneers in the intuition development movement, having worked since 1977 with organizations like the Center for Applied Intuition, The Institute for the Study of Conscious Evolution, and The Intuition Network. Her work has been used as part of the curriculum at Coach U, The Coaches Training Institute, Holos University, the Spiritual Psychology program at University of Santa Monica, and the University of Johannesburg Graduate program in Business Leadership. Additionally, she works with The Arlington Institute, a group of futurists in Washington, DC. She has also been on the faculty of The Kaiser Institute, teaching in their Intuition Fellowship program.

A popular author, lecturer, counselor, and trainer, Penney specializes in intuition and sensitivity development, skillful perception, personal energy and frequency training, dream work, and future trends. She travels widely, has led spiritual tours, and has counseled tens of thousands of people worldwide. She also has worked with trance medium Kevin Ryerson, who gained wide popularity through his connection with actress Shirley MacLaine.

Penney is the author of *Frequency: The Power of Personal Vibration, The Intuitive Way: The Definitive Guide to Increasing Your Awareness, Dream Dictionary for Dummies, Dreams for Dummies,* and *The Present Moment: a Daybook of Clarity and Intuition.* Penney has also contributed to or been featured in numerous books by other authors and in magazines.

Q. What experiences put you on your spiritual path?

A. It was a gradual unfolding. I was always curious about the mysteries. In high school, I began reading books like *The Psychic Sense*, by Edgar Cayce and *Psychic Discoveries Behind the Iron Curtain*, by Sheila Ostrander. After attending the University of Cincinnati, I moved to New York City where I worked as a designer while reading books by mediums like Jane Roberts, Ruth Montgomery, and Taylor Caldwell and studying with the famous ghost hunter Hans Holtzer. I then moved to Los Angeles to attend California Institute of the Arts, where I got a degree in an experimental program called Social Design. In it, we did projects like: redesign the elevator so people would talk to each other inside, redesign the doctor-patient relationship, and redesign funerals. This taught me how to think intuitively. After Cal Arts, I moved to Marin County, north of San Francisco, California, where the New Age movement was taking off. This was the mid-1970s.

I suddenly found myself in the midst of an array of fascinating classes that I soaked up like a sponge—from nutrition, to tai chi, to shamanism, to clairvoyance development. With my background in graphic design, I was visual already and by studying meditation and clairvoyance development, I discovered that the images I received in my imagination actually meant something! I could pick up information about a person through symbols. I learned that my dreams, which I'd always thought were ordinary, were bringing me visions, precognitive information, and spiritual teachings. This period was marked by a rapid recovery—through reading, taking classes, meditating, and keeping a daily journal—of information I felt I already knew. Eventually, I began to teach metaphysical classes and do intuitive readings. I then joined the Center for Applied Intuition founded by Dr.

> "I had stayed away from the church, vowing not to even say the word God until I had a clearer idea of what it meant."

INTUITIVE

William H. Kautz, a scientist from Stanford Research Institute.

Dr. Kautz had designed an interesting process he called "intuitive consensus." He gathered a team of accurate intuitives and created various sets of questions, often aimed at finding new angles for scientific research or insights for corporations. Each intuitive then independently did a reading, answering the questions. Dr. Kautz organized the responses, paying special attention to the common elements, and created a report. It was through this service that I first was invited to work in Japan in 1984, and I have been involved there ever since.

> "Once I became activated, I started learning from inside, from my 'inner teacher.'"

Q. How did these experiences change you?

A. I received information through readings with trance mediums Dollee Campbell and Kevin Ryerson (who I worked and taught with for four years) about my past lives, in some cases with specific details that I was able to verify through research. Kevin's entities said they had seen me teach before and that I had a great deal of experience spiritually. This was long before I thought of myself as qualified to teach anyone about anything, but it gave me confidence. I later learned that I'd had many lives in the church as a minister and missionary and that I was still operating from a similar motivation. In this life, I had stayed away from the church, vowing not to even say the word God until I had a clearer idea of what it meant.

Then, when I was about thirty, I saw Franco Zeffirelli's movie about Jesus. When it got to the part where John baptizes Jesus, I started sobbing. Jesus began coming to me in my dreams and I discovered in another reading that I had

PENNY PEIRCE

177

worked with John the Baptist. I felt like parts of me were reintegrating. Learning about my past lives encouraged me to move ahead and eventually teach spirituality. In general, I developed strong faith in my dreams, inner motivations, and insights. I felt I was being guided, as one thing after another opened before me, and each thing seemed to make sense.

Q. What changes are you noticing about your life and the world?

A. A large part of my early motivation for doing intuitive and spiritual work came from my past lives as a Christian in which I felt noble by serving and sacrificing for God. Not long ago, I realized I didn't want to serve from this motivation any-more. Instead, I realized I wanted to have more fun. So, I dabbled with art but stayed in spiritual work because I con-tinued to be fascinated with the higher realms. For a while, I lived without a motive and experienced disillusionment concerning lack of purpose. Eventually I saw how this was necessary for me to complete one major life stage and move into another, where my frequency could be much higher and I could understand Spirit in an even broader, more universal way. Now I see that service is often what I naturally choose when I feel totally free and don't need to make my life hap-pen through personal will power.

Q. What changes are others noticing about you?

A. My father, who was originally trained as an engineer, said before he died, "Penney, I don't always know what you're talking about. I know certain words to mean one thing but you use them entirely differently. At least you're consistent and I admire your dedication." I think in my early years, I was so focused on building my character and remembering old knowledge that I was probably pretty hard to live with. I'm sure my family thought I was off my rocker, since they figured I'd most likely become a corporate president like my father. After many years, my family and friends tell me I've become much softer.

INTUITIVE

Q. What has been the most challenging part of your path?

A. Having intimate relationships! I was always trying to face my fears and tell the truth. That doesn't go over well with most people, especially when they aren't focused on the spiritual path to the same degree. As a result, most of my personal growth has been done on my own. The work I've done in relationships tends to be about the common traits, especially the negative ones, that I share with others. For example, if angry people show up in my life and upset me, I realize I must have that in myself too and, thus, I need to clear the underlying causes of the anger from myself. This work is helpful, but not always peaceful. Now that I'm older, I'm experiencing much more peace in my relationships and in myself. And I really love co-creating with others.

Q. What is your earliest memory? Why do you remember it?

A. At around age one, I remember playing with another kid in a swimming pool and having a great time. I recall serious things as well. For example, when I was four, I carried around a large book, pretending to be a professor teaching a class of imaginary students. I also remember thinking, *I was born and now I'll have to die.* I was upset because I felt trapped. I remember my mother telling me that the body was "just a shell," and when you die, your soul leaves it behind. For years I thought the soul was shaped like a peanut shell. I suppose even then, I was thinking about Spirit.

Q. Who are your mentors? What have you learned from them?

A. I was fortunate to learn from very good teachers. Joan Grigsby taught me a tremendous amount about meditation, visualization, concentration, and intuition in her clairvoyance development classes. Kevin Ryerson, the trance medium who worked with Shirley MacLaine, is like a soul brother who opened me to new realms as we did readings and taught together. Dollee Campbell, through her past life readings, helped encourage me to live my true life purpose. Bill Kautz,

PENNY PEIRCE

179

> "At our soul level, we are perfect. All we need to do is listen to and act on ideas that emanate from there."

the Director of the Center for Applied Intuition, gave me an opportunity to work with other professional intuitives in a very grounded way. Bob Boyll, a shaman, introduced me to working with sound and ceremony, and Bob Rasmussen, a spiritual healer, affirmed the reality of the higher energy realms by dissolving a tumor and mending a broken bone I had—in a matter of minutes.

Once I became activated, I started learning from inside, from my "inner teacher." I didn't read other teachers' work or take many classes. Now I read books by authors like Eckhart Tolle and find I've been saying the same thing. Recently, I heard Zen Buddhist Baker Roshi speak. He said certain phrases that helped shift my awareness by a few degrees, and suddenly new connections were made and I had important "ahas." This is the way I now find most of my learning comes—through subtle changes of perspective and interesting new combinations of concepts. And often these things come from the mouths of friends and family.

Q. What is the greatest challenge facing society?

A. Fear. We believe suffering is normal, that life has to be hard, that we won't get what we really want. These beliefs contribute to personal and cultural negativity that creates negative, dysfunctional mores and structures. When new possibilities show up, we often belittle or derail them because we're so accustomed to lack and strife. However, deep down, we harbor hope. More and more of us are choosing love and truth now, as the frequency on the planet increases. As we do, we spread this new reality to others. Then problems that looked impossible to resolve turn around. Changing our inner reality from fear-based to love-based changes our outer world. We still need to take action to ease people's suffering, just as we

INTUITIVE

have always done, especially in America where philanthropy is strong and we can influence other nations to do the same. I do think that now, though, higher consciousness is streamlining our efforts.

Q. What advice would you give someone just starting on his or her spiritual path?

A. I think mindfulness, or what Buddhists call "The Path of Inquiry" is very important. When you notice what you're noticing each moment and ask, "Why am I noticing this?" it helps you get in touch with your deepest self and truest motives. It eventually helps you clear away the clutter of other people's ideas and false programming. For example, you can notice when you feel fear, which contracts your body, and joy, which relaxes and expands it. When you're mindful, you can choose between these two feeling states, which is the path to freedom. At our soul level, we are perfect. All we need to do is listen to and act on ideas that emanate from there, moment by moment. Of course, the quieter you become, the easier it is to hear those messages. In the velvety silence, you can easily connect with inner wisdom. And then, when you put your attention in the outside world, you'll find yourself in everything and will no longer feel separate, but connected to it all. So turn off your cell phone and really listen!

Q. What are your practices for connecting to your higher purpose?

A. I look for the patterns in my thoughts and experiences to uncover hidden messages from my deeper self. I also work with my day and night dreams to see what the less visible parts of me are doing. When I do intuitive readings for people, I go into a very deep state of communion that allows me to experience compassion much more easily. Also, when I garden, I get into a trance-like flow and

> **"When we shift, the world will shift."**

PENNY PEIRCE

move with the rhythms of nature. Occasionally, I can be still enough to actually meditate. But mostly, I try to be aware of beauty, awe, and gratitude for being alive.

Q. How do you use these practices when you get out of balance?

A. People's inconsiderate behavior, such as rudeness or loud cell phones, can irritate me and my body contracts. I try to notice the contraction and let everything just be the way it is for a moment. I then re-center and return to my home frequency by breathing, moving, and/or distracting myself with a better feeling. My home frequency—the way I really like to feel—is cheerful and playful, warm, buttery, enthusiastic, and engaged. When I feel like this, my true self flows through and I can give others the space to be obnoxious or chaotic without having it disturb me. Another thing that helps is remembering that our Mother Earth's body embraces everything from pollutants, volcanoes, and storms to nesting birds and peaceful valleys. If the Earth can do it, so can I.

Q. How do you balance planning with remaining open to opportunity?

A. I combine planning with free flow. When I arrange a trip or a project, for example, I first zoom out to see the big picture. I notice the feeling my body gets about the whole thing and where the sticking points might be. If something feels off, I drop down to the specific view, put attention on the details, and perhaps adjust the sequence of events. Then I zoom out again to check if things become smoother. In this way, I rock back and forth between the broad overview and the specific tasks. It's really not possible anymore to lock in plans. The planet and the physical plane are just vibrating too rapidly and the flow is constantly shifting us around. We have to be ready to change on a dime. So, as a strong "J" on Myers-Briggs, I get a handle on things and then let go to watch them form. It's fun to see how they unfold.

INTUITIVE

Q. If you received $100,000, how would you spend it?

A. The money would cause my imagination to expand. I would hire assistants so I could be free to do other things. I would create media products to reach more people with information about the Intuition Age. I would buy a home to give me a stable base. The house would have a view and be out in nature because being surrounded by beauty supports me in maintaining my center, accessing higher dimensions, and staying creative.

Q. If you had thirty seconds with someone in an elevator, what three things would you tell the person to do to be joyful, peaceful, and whole?

A. Drop into yourself, relax, and find a way to be entertained by whatever is occurring in your reality bubble. Right now, you have what you asked for a little while ago, so use it to improve yourself. And be ready for surprise. The next thought that comes to you is going to be really interesting!

Q. What books or resources have helped you the most? Why?

A. These authors have had an impact on me: Jane Roberts and Seth, Edgar Cayce, David Spangler, Taylor Caldwell, Jess Stearn, Sri Aurobindo and The Mother, Sri Nisargadatta, Fritz Perls, Barbara Hand Clow, J.G. Bennett, John Anthony West, Joseph Chilton Pearce, Lyall Watson, Barry Holston Lopez, The Abraham-Hicks material, Rainer Maria Rilke, and Helen Schucman and William Thetford.

I particularly resonate with Sri Nisargadatta, Sri Aurobindo, and The Mother. For example, in *The Mind of The Cells*, The Mother talks about going down into her body to clear the fear that's been programmed into the cells. Her description of the consciousness in her body is amazingly similar to what I experience. Nisargadatta's dialogue in *I Am That* directly transports me into his state of consciousness. I am fascinated by this ability to keep the consciousness alive in the writ-

PENNY PEIRCE

ten word. It's a powerful spiritual practice to create art with authentic connection. A single line of music or poetry, or a painting, or scene in a movie has the power to transform me. I try to imbue my writing with this same aliveness.

Now I'm inspired by innovators like Dean Kamen, who pull ideas out of the ethers and make them real. My father was an engineer and my mother was an architect, so I've always been interested in elegant solutions that save time and energy by solving multiple problems at once. Once you learn to live according to universal principles, the next step is harnessing imagination and creativity.

Q. What would you like to be written on your tombstone?

A. I don't want to be buried and have a tombstone. I believe being buried makes it harder to let go of the body and release into Spirit. When my father died, I scattered his ashes in the four directions. I would like the same done with mine so I can be left in beautiful nature spots around the world. I've even thought about having a park where trees could be planted over me, creating a living graveyard rather than one full of death markers. Honestly, I don't care much about being remembered. Whatever I write will be studied for a while, then fade as other things naturally eclipse the points of view. When I had the past life readings, it was interesting to see how the strands of my previous lives had woven together to help me do what I'm doing now. I feel privileged to be able to be the continuance of all of us, as it were. So I'd be pleased if I could leave something behind for my next life to find and carry on!

Q. Anything else?

A. It's so important to relax and trust. The process of life is evolving us so we don't need to generate everything by ourselves. We do need to watch for messages and take action based on inspiration. Doing things from a joyful state is part of the new reality bubbling up in our consciousness. When we shift into this higher frequency reality, our lives change for the better. We find balance by being in the moment and doing what we're called to do. As people who are waking up, this is our work, and it is critically important right now—to stabilize the new Intuition Age perception. When we shift, the world will shift.

And we need to follow the flow of inspiration, because it does ebb at times. For example, I wrote my first three books because the subject material totally fascinated me. Then I stopped because no new information excited me. The down-time allowed me to have fun and learn new things so the next new wave of ideas could surface. When we act from inspiration, we don't worry so much. Worry causes us to either push to get things done or give up and become lazy. Part of staying in touch with inspiration is working with our dream life. At night, and even in daydreams, we hone the ideas and insights that want to materialize and we teach ourselves. I think we must stay alert to everything that happens because it's the greater self, or the divine part of ourselves, talking to us. And if we guide ourselves by this flow, we'll achieve our life purpose and destiny.

PENNY PEIRCE

"There is only one happiness in this life, to love and be loved."

\- George Sand

*"I chose to come here and "do stupid human tricks"
to learn and grow."*
Linda Potter, Author of *If God Would Only Give Me a Sign*
Editor of *BellaSpark Magazine*

Linda Potter is a professional public speaker, published author, licensed spiritual counselor, and managing editor of *BellaSpark Magazine*. She has interviewed numerous human potential experts including Wayne Dyer, Deepak Chopra, Alan Cohen, and Dr. Joe Dispenza. Linda teaches classes on meditation and affirmative prayer and conducts workshops on the quantum physics/spirituality connection through the Whole Life Center for Spiritual Living in Fort Collins, Colorado. Her educational background includes a master's degree in theatre and a bachelor's degree in speech and theatre arts. Currently, she and her husband live in Windsor, Colorado

Q. What experiences put you on your spiritual path?
A. I truly believe that you don't have to suffer a crucifixion in order to experience a resurrection, but, ironically, it helps. Once you've hit bottom, the only direction you can go is up. Divorce was that kind of "hit bottom" experience for me. It was on my way back up that I found New Thought and Religious Science. It was a new and different way of looking at my relationship with God, and yet there was something comfortable and familiar about it—like I'd come home.

The metaphysical teachings were so nurturing that I immersed myself in courses and, in fewer than five years, became a licensed Religious Science Practitioner and an interim minister. Understanding that I was whole, perfect, and complete just as I was helped me embrace myself fully. I accepted my psychic abilities, which I had pulled away from as a child because they frightened me, e.g., seeing people who had passed on, knowing about future events, and so on. Looking back, it was all divine timing.

Q. How did these experiences change you?

A. When I realized that life is an illusion—as the *Leap!* filmmakers say—I saw that I could redefine my reality. As Wayne Dyer says, "Change your thoughts, change your life." As a result, I gave myself permission to let go of relationships, work styles, and habits that no longer served me. Now, I'm more even-keeled and patient. I don't push into tasks anymore or feel the tension, fear, and urgency to get them done.

Q. What has been the most challenging part of your path?

A. The most challenging part is how my relationships have evolved. People I was close to for years, including some family members, are not in my life in the same way. I still love these people and maintain contact with them, but our paths have gone in different directions. We need this time and space to grow as individuals. Of course, new people have come into my life. So I feel the joy of blossoming new relationships and the grief of leaving old ones.

Q. What changes are you noticing about your life and the world?

A. I recognize that we are all connected, that I'm part of something greater. This awareness gives me flow, ease, and compassion in my life. In the past, I agonized over the atrocities taking place in the world. Now I see my responsibility as holding higher consciousness for peace and love without needing to resolve all injustices single-handedly. This realization helps me accept what is without giving up hope for what can be.

Q. What changes are others noticing about you?

A. My children are my greatest sounding board. They say I'm more patient, understanding, and compassionate. When they used to come to me for advice, I would try to steer them

AUTHOR

in the direction *I* thought they should go. Now I am able to provide support and discuss options without an agenda. This openness came after a lot of forgiveness work that helped me release past resentments. One of my favorite quotes is, "Resentment is like taking poison and expecting the other person to die." (anonymous) My life now is about honoring the divinity within everyone and letting go.

Q. What is your earliest memory? Why do you remember it?

A. At age six, I was sitting in church with my mother on Easter. A light ray shined on me through the window and I heard a voice, which I knew was God, say, "No matter what, you are loved." Frightened, I turned to my mother and asked, "Did you see that?" to which she replied, "I didn't see anything." For years I wondered if it had really happened or if it was just my imagination. Thirty-six years later, at church for my son's Confirmation, I found myself watching a hand-shaped cloud that had suddenly appeared in one of the skylights above the sanctuary. As I watched, the "hand" opened, shining a ray of light on me that was so bright, I had to close my eyes. Again, I heard the words, "You are loved." Crying, I turned to my husband and asked, "Did you see that?" to which he answered, "Yes." There was no denying the experience this time, and being able to share it with my husband made it even more meaningful.

Q. Who are your mentors? What have you learned from them?

A. John Randolph Price, best selling author and speaker, who first opened my eyes to New Thought and metaphysics. Nothing seems too far outside the box for him. He has written about everything, from angels and abundance to wellness and world peace. His books encouraged me to be an open-minded, lifetime spiritual seeker.

Other mentors include: Ernest Holmes, founder of Religious Science, who developed our thought system around the science of mind and spirit; Paul Polak, founder of International

LINDA POTTER

Development Enterprises (IDE) and D-REV, who has dedicated his life to ending poverty through teaching farmers in developing countries how to invest in success; and my husband, children, and grandchildren, who constantly remind me that unconditional love is possible.

Q. What is the greatest challenge facing society?

A. Awakening to the truth of oneness so we can see God in everything and everyone. If we had this sense of interconnectedness, we wouldn't have our current problems. Through embracing oneness, we would understand that everything we do to another, we also do to ourselves.

Q. What advice would you give someone just starting his or her spiritual path?

A. Pay attention to your inner guidance, for it will lead you to what you need—sometimes when you least expect it, in ways you could never have predicted. For example, I first discovered John Randolph Price's teachings at a yard sale where I found his book, *The Angels Within Us*, on a table in the back of a garage. I bought it and couldn't stop reading it. I've just written a book called, *If God Would Only Give Me a Sign*, in which I use everyday signs such as "Open For Business" and "Fog Conditions May Exist" to discuss inner guidance. We often ask God to give us dramatic signs when, in reality, we already have all the signs we need. We simply have to notice.

Q. What are your practices for connecting to your higher purpose?

A. Every day, I meditate, usually in my hot tub overlooking the beautiful lake behind my home. I connect to my higher power and ask questions, vent frustrations, or just be. My work as a spiritual counselor and managing editor for *BellaSpark Magazine* helps me "pray without ceasing." (Paul, 1 Thessalonians 5:17) When your vocation is an expression of who you are, your life becomes a prayer.

Q. How do you use these practices when you get out of balance?

A. I monitor what I think and say because thoughts and words have power. Since I am aware, I catch myself sooner when I fall into drama. When I need to spend time venting, I get into my hot tub sanctuary and set the timer for twenty minutes. Symbolically, I am stepping into hot water and emerging calm when the churning waters stop.

Q. How do you balance planning with remaining open to opportunity?

A. I still like to plan, but now I look at it differently. My role is to set a clear intention and then let God fill in the details. With this approach, I am more open to spontaneity and less attached to outcome. This approach frees me to realize the universe's larger vision.

Q. If you received $100,000, how would you spend it?

A. I would use the money to celebrate life. I believe in tithing to my spiritual source and that would be my first priority. I also have a few favorite charities, like IDE. Then I would find wonderful, creative ways to spend the rest. A trip to Maui, Hawaii would be nice, and I'd love to self-publish some books.

Q. If you had thirty seconds with someone in an elevator, what three things would you tell the person to do to be joyful, peaceful, and whole?

A. We do a disservice when we try to distill a person's spiritual journey into three steps. I would invite him or her to join me for a cup of tea and conversation. Our talk would focus on finding God within, because peace, joy, and love all emanate from this place. I learn my greatest lessons from everyday experiences like spending time with my grandson and discovering the world through his eyes. In this playful, open state, I see divine signs all around me.

LINDA POTTER

Q. What books or resources have helped you the most? Why?

A. The greatest resource is spending time with others on the spiritual path. There's something magical about human inter- action. We discover insights we wouldn't have on our own. Personally, I am a speaker first and a writer second. When I give a talk, my soul fills because I get to share what I know and see people light up. In turn, I learn from their questions and comments. In this way, we empower each other.

Q. What would you like to be written on your tombstone?

A. In the spirit of Pierre Teilhard de Chardin, I would like these words written: "She was a spiritual being who celebrated the human experience." I embrace my human experience with- out any regrets. I chose to come here and "do stupid human tricks" to learn and grow. If I deny an experience, it will just keep returning until I integrate it. Embrace life in all its fac- ets!

Q. Anything else?

A. Spiritual growth is about the journey. There are plenty of signs from God on the path to enlightenment: "Stay on Path," "Yield" to God, know when to "Stop" and rethink your direction, "Proceed When Clear," and always remember that when "Help (is) Wanted," you simply need to "Inquire With- in."

AUTHOR

"My creative fire connects me to God."
Rev. Dr. Christina A. Rose, Universal Life Church

Religions are a passion for Christina. She has studied all over the world to explore how different cultures worship. She received her doctorate of divinity in 2007, and has continued to work towards a greater understanding between people in regards to their spirituality. She is currently working online using the world of Second Life to further her teachings and to help people find their own personal spiritual path. She can be contacted there under the avatar name of Aislinn Jaerls, or through email at redtudorrose@gmail.com.

Q. What experiences put you on your spiritual path?

A. I found the book, *The Truth About Witchcraft*, by Scott Cunningham in a metaphysical store during a high school field trip. I hid it under my bed knowing my devout Christian parents would disapprove. The book opened a new world to me. After studying Wiccan and pagan beliefs, I went on to practice Shinto (The Way of the Gods), the former state religion of Japan, which draws upon Buddhism, animism, and shamanism. While walking through Westminster Abbey four years ago, my Scottish ancestors called me home to Paganism. On the British Isles, blending Celtic Paganism, Christianity, and shamanism is a way of life.

Q. How did these experiences change you?

A. Rolling up my sleeves to worship with people from different faiths has given me a loving acceptance of all religions. I see the beauty in every path and how that beauty enhances my own spiritual journey. As a larger spirituality took hold of my heart, I could not help but evolve into a different person.

Q. What changes are you noticing about your life and the world?

A. I have a heightened appreciation of God/Goddess and the natural world. For example, I used to complain about shoveling the driveway or driving on icy roads after a snowstorm. Now I celebrate the magnificence of the snow covering the mountains. In fact, I embrace everything that happens. Accepting what life brings makes it easier to cope in the world. As a say to my son, "It is what it is."

Q. What changes are you noticing about your life and the world?

A. My life partner, Kimberly, and my son say I am happier. I am more forgiving of human faults and relate to people on a deeper level. I even became a spiritual counselor. I could not have done this work without adopting a broader spirituality. By encompassing different faiths, I can see people as they are without dogma getting in the way.

Q. What has been the most challenging part of your path?

A. The human aspect is the most challenging part of any spiritual path. Our psyches have trouble understanding that there are paths outside our own. Religion is not a cookie cutter. Every person's spiritual experience is unique. For example, twenty Christians listening to the same sermon will each take away something different. To cultivate greater unity, we need to walk in another's shoes, seeing God/Goddess through his or her eyes.

Q. What is your earliest memory? Why do you remember it?

A. At age four, I saw a ghost hovering outside my brother's room. I yelled to my parents, who came and assured me there was no such thing as ghosts. After this experience, I felt less alone in the house. I had a greater awareness of the world around me and more questions regarding the afterlife. My parents' morbid sense of humor eased this tension with annual trips to the graveyard to find the oldest gravestones.

Q. Who are your mentors? What have you learned from them?

A. Reverend Koichi Barrish, chief priest (*gūji*) of the Tsubaki Grand Shrine of America. I admire him because he overcame adversity to become the first non-Japanese Shinto priest. He is powerful and effective due to his larger-than-life stature and gruff form of tough love. My partner and I worked at the shrine during New Year's—the most important Shinto holiday—and I could feel his commanding presence everywhere. I don't have other mentors because my spiritual path has been one of self-discovery.

Q. What is the greatest challenge facing society?

A. Our inability to overcome personal differences and get along. In tribal societies, people had to get along in order to survive. Now we just leave when situations get difficult. For example, if you don't like your pastor, you find another church. We hurt only ourselves when we fail to build common ground. It's time to get out of our own little boxes and befriend people from different cultures, classes, and races. Only then will world peace be possible.

Q. What advice would you give someone just starting his or her spiritual path?

A. Study many different faiths. When you find one you like, worship there but continue learning about other religions. This exploration will help you better connect to people, the world, and your own spiritual path. You will discover universal themes and integrate different practices into your own faith to make your path richer. For example, in our house, we celebrate "Christmayulika," a combination of Christmas, Hanukkah, and Yule observance.

Q. What are your practices for connecting to your higher purpose?

A. I connect to God/Goddess through service and creative projects. When I counsel others or make crafts like prayer beads,

I feel close to God/Goddess and my higher self. I'm not one to sit and mediate quietly. I put the divine into everything I do.

Q. How do you use these practices when you get out of balance?

A. When someone criticizes or cuts me off, I take a deep breath and say, "It's okay." I know that in most cases, the person didn't mean to harm me. He or she isn't self-aware enough in that moment to know what's happening. I just let it go because I'm sure I have done the same in the past.

Q. How do you balance planning with remaining open to opportunity?

A. I am chaos embodied. The only scheduling I do is around work and shared use of the car. When I overstructure the day, it snuffs out my creative fire. If I can't create, I die a little inside. I breathe the spark of inspiration into all my endeavors, e.g., kimono making, counseling, volunteering, etc.

Q. If you received $100,000, how would you spend it?

A. I would support the arts in public schools, fund the food bank at Sister Carmen's Community Center, pay my taxes, and then go clothes shopping—my form of retail therapy.

Q. If you had thirty seconds with someone in an elevator, what three things would you tell the person to do to be joyful, peaceful, and whole?

A. Let things go. Releasing the past frees you to embrace the present. Find your own connection to God. Worship in a way that works for you. To thine own self be true. Honor yourself by living your unique purpose. Love each other. Always give love, even when someone cannot receive it.

Q. What books or resources have helped you the most? Why?

A. The best resource is love. I found the love of my life and we have done more together than I ever could have done by myself. Read as many books as you can. Start with one that teaches you about the world's religions. I read one to my son when he was four and he has matured into a young man who appreciates other faiths and cultures.

Q. What would you like to be written on your tombstone?
A. I am going to have a Viking funeral with a giant bonfire and towering flames. My partner's and my ashes will be blended and spread over southern Scotland. My passing will be a time of great celebration as I join my ancestors in the afterlife.

Q. Anything else?
A. Paganism is an ancient religion deeply rooted in nature. Pagans worship the Horned God (sun and masculinity) and the Triple Goddess (moon and femininity), who has aspects of mother, maiden, and crone. Pagans follow the Wheel of the Year, celebrating eight holidays known as Sabbats. These Sabbats revolve around relations between the God and Goddess. The God impregnates the Goddess during Beltane (May Eve), then dies on Samhain (Halloween), the beginning of the New Year. He is reborn on Yule (Winter Solstice), which represents both the birth of the son and the return of the sun. The son becomes the Goddess' lover again on Beltane and the cycle of life continues. Wiccans are neo-pagans who practice nature magic and gather in covens to perform more structured rituals.

REV. DR. CHRISTINA A. ROSE

"Let the body speak."
- Jean-Pierre Barral, D.O.

"Listen and trust your inner knowing."
Suzanne Scurlock-Durana, Author of *Full Body Presence*
CranioSacral Instructor and Therapist

For more than twenty-five years, Suzanne has taught and mentored in the area of conscious awareness and its relationship to the healing process. She has developed a unique approach to energy, presence, grounding and integrative exercises taught in the *Healing from the Core* program, which includes a six-level training course and complementary audio series. She is passionate about teaching people practical skills that allow them to feel the joy of being present in each moment of their lives without burning out. To that end, she has just completed a book and companion CD, *Full-Body Presence: Explorations, Connections* and *More to Experience Present Moment Awareness.*

Since 1986, she has been a certified instructor of CranioSacral Therapy (CST) and SomatoEmotional Release with The Upledger Institute, teaching both nationally and internationally. She is also on the faculty at Esalen Institute. Known for her honest, grounded, nurturing manner, Suzanne assists others in going to the heart of their healing process. She is adept at weaving together mind, body, and spirit to create a unique environment where profound healing can occur.

A sought after speaker in her field, Suzanne inspires healthcare practitioners, coaches, teachers, and caregivers around the world to stay energized using her life changing tools for stress management and full body presence. She has authored numerous articles and thousands visit her blog, Presence Matters at http://massagemag.com/massage-blog/presence-matters. She has a private practice in Reston, Virginia.

Q. What experiences put you on your spiritual path?

A. I have had a series of life changing experiences that put me on my path. One of the earliest was at age ten when I was walking home from church on a clear summer's night. I suddenly was filled with an overwhelming sense of being one with everything around me—trees, sky, and air. It was deeply inspiring. That experience left me with the clear sense of connection to life that is everyone's birthright. I have made it my life's work to bring that felt sense of connection to everyone I can.

Later, as an adult in my late twenties, I had another spiritual wake-up call. I was in a meditation training where we practiced a series of mental and physical exercises designed to allow the mind to drop away and the soul's voice to emerge. As we did the final exercise, I found myself filling with a golden fluid, starting from my toes. As it reached my eyes, tears of joy emerged and spilled down my cheeks. We all lay on the floor to complete the exercise and huge rushes of energy started to move through me like a freight train. As the energy hit points of compression in my body, it was excruciating. When the compressed places opened up, and the energy moved on, it was ecstatic. Although it was a lot of sensation, and much of it not comfortable, I somehow trusted, relaxed, and let it flow through me.

As the rushes of energy slowed down and dissipated, my hands were still buzzing with energy. I had a passing thought about why they were still vibrating when everything else had quieted and, as though in response to my question, I heard a deep, gentle voice say, "How many more times must I tell you that what you are to do is with your hands?" I knew in that moment that I had been given a life direction and it felt right. It eventually led me to CranioSacral Therapy and my work with Full Body Presence.

Q. How did these experiences change you?

A. First, let me say that my father was a huge role model for me as a child. I adored my dad. I thought the sun and moon set over him. Since he was a very good linear, rational thinker, I pushed myself to be as well, even though my natural tendency is to be more heart and feeling centered. The early spiritual experiences I just described expanded my perceptual lens and brought me back to my heart and the cellular intelligence of the body. They showed me that not everything could be explained with the logical mind. While reason and focus get us from point A to B, it is not as important as the Great Mystery that deeply nourishes and feeds us moment to moment in our lives.

Q. What changes are you noticing about your life and the world?

A. When I am fully present, I flow with life. I see events more clearly and things come to me with ease. When I get ahead of myself, I do not communicate as clearly or operate as efficiently. A perfect example happened several years ago, as I was packing for a trip to Esalen, where I teach classes every summer for a month. I had so many details to handle that I was focusing harder and harder as my departure time approached. I could tell that I was starting to do what I call "getting ahead of myself," trying to remember everything. Then one of my presenters came over so I could evaluate her presentation of the grounding and filling exploration for certification. As she walked me through the twenty-minute exercise, I found my energy sinking back into my body—into my spine, sit bones, and feet—as I invited nourishing sensations to fill me. Then all my to-do lists vanished as the stray details I had forgotten gently floated into my consciousness.

This exercise brought me so fully into the present that all the information I needed just came. Now I know that when I am fully present and still lack clarity, it's a sign that it's not time to make a decision yet. And when I'm not fully present and try to rush or delay the decision, I know the outcome will be less than optimal. I will have missed important information.

Q. What changes are others noticing about you?

A. My mother, sister, and some lifelong friends would say I am softer, more accepting, and more lighthearted. The linear left brain gets dry after a while. So I learned to let it go and stay in the moment. When I am present, I can laugh at situations and myself.

Q. What has been the most challenging part of your path?

A. Keeping balance between my feminine and masculine sides in my closest personal relationships. I am a woman who grew up with a straightforward, tell-it-like-it-is and go-for-the-goal attitude. This is how I saw the world and resolved issues. So I had to learn how to slow down, to allow myself to be receptive, and to let my natural openheartedness shine through. My friends would say I am fun to be around, that I listen well and share my thoughts and feelings, and that I give great hugs. I enjoy things like singing and dancing, having a good time, and relaxing and enjoying life. But they also would tell you that I always have an eye on my next creative endeavor. So the balance between being and doing is a constant internal conversation for me.

Q. What is your earliest memory? Why do you remember it?

A. I remember being in the sunlight and walking down the sidewalk next to someone larger whose finger I held in my hand. There were lots of beautiful flowers and a white picket fence. I must have been a toddler, because this description matches where I lived my first year of life. I also remember looking into my brother's crib when I was a year-and-a-half old and recognizing him. I thought, *What are you doing here?* We had a very deep, old connection that made us close, but extremely competitive, in childhood.

Q. Who are your mentors? What have you learned from them?

A. I have had the honor of learning from many excellent teachers. My two greatest female mentors are Emilie Conrad and Susan Harper, who embody living in the flow of life. Emilie's Continuum Movement work has expanded my consciousness and human beingness. She helped me fully connect with my body and sensuality. She also showed me how to play with sound and breath. Susan Harper's work with conscious awareness and the embodiment process continues to help me grow. She has been a friend since high school and actually introduced me to Emilie when they were first working together.

My greatest male mentor is Dr. John Upledger, developer of CranioSacral Therapy. He taught me how to listen to the body with my whole being, through my hands. He also taught me how to dialogue with all parts of the body, which translated into my ability to dialogue with all of life. When I dialogue with someone's system in a clear, authentic way, it can lead to a life changing outcome. For example, through touch and talking with the damaged area of a client's liver or shoulder, we can change its cellular structure so that it opens to whatever healing is possible.

There are practitioners who facilitate this type of change without talking. But even excellent body workers fall into the trap of being right on with their hands and way off in the stories they make up about what they find. These stories can belittle the healing process and take the client down a path that isn't real.

So Dr. John adamantly says, "Do not make assumptions about what you think is happening in another person's system. Ask the person's body." This approach not only helps the client's inner knowing get on board, but also encourages the client to take ownership of his or her own healing process. The person leaves the session with a greater sense of his or her own wisdom and healing capacity, rather than being awed by how much I might know.

SUZANNE SCURLOCK-DURANA

Other mentors include:
Rosalyn Bruyere D.D., founder of the Healing Light Center Church, who taught me early on about hands-on energy work and indigenous tribal healing traditions. .

Dr. Fritz Smith, founder of Zero Balancing, who taught me about aligning energy with the body's physical structure, the bones.

Susan Trout Ph.D., founder of the Center for Attitudinal Healing, who helped me identify my limiting beliefs and work through them.

Q. What is the greatest challenge facing society?

A. Many people find it difficult to feel what's inside them due to the amount of external information we are bombarded with and the speed at which we are expected to respond. We need to shed some of the rules we learned about acceptable behavior and reclaim our connection to our internal world. This connection involves deeply listening to and translating the signals we receive. Some signals are loud. For example, when you are in danger, your gut will tell you to get out. If you ignore the warning, as I did when I was seventeen and didn't know any better, you could end up getting strangled, as I did. Sometimes the signals are subtle. To hear them clearly, you must be still and pay close attention. Some people don't have a clue how to listen. Others don't trust what they hear and second-guess themselves constantly. But learning the skills of inner listening, feeling your heart, and trusting what you feel will assist you in making the most of your gifts. And knowing what your heart wants to birth creatively is vital to happiness.

Q. What advice would you give someone just starting his or her spiritual path?

A. Learn to listen to and trust your inner knowing—that part of

AUTHOR, CRANIOSACRAL INSTRUCTOR AND THERAPIST

you that is connected to God and the Universal All. When you make a deep connection to the Universal All, it doesn't matter what your spiritual path is. You'll be guided and fed by that connection, which is present in the roots of all faiths: Buddhism, Taoism, Islam... That's why I don't believe everyone has to accept Jesus as Lord and Savior, even though I was raised that way. I left the Baptist church when I was seventeen because I realized its limits and knew there had to be more. So I began studying Eastern spiritual traditions and meditation, indigenous traditions, and the origins of other religions. In my experience, there are many paths to connection with God or the Universal All, and when you are deeply connected, it feels the same no matter what your path.

Q. What are your practices for connecting to your higher purpose?

A. One of my favorite practices is cultivating a feeling of gratitude in my daily life. I feel gratitude that I'm here right now in this moment. When I am grateful, my heart opens, my belly relaxes, and my mind slows down. I also like to start each day with some type of movement such as walking. I get up early and walk in the forest and around the lake behind my house. This practice fills me up and reminds me of the beauty of all life. It also wakes up my system and gets energy flowing through me.

My primary practice centers around connecting to healthy resources, such as taking my awareness down into the rich energy field of the Earth, enjoying a deep, easy breath to connect me to the air around me, and expanding my awareness into the heavens above. My entire original audio series, *Healing From the Core: A Journey Home to Ourselves*, consists of multiple ways of connecting to healthy, unconditional, internal and external resources that anyone can tap into on a moment's notice.

SUZANNE SCURLOCK-DURANA

Q. How do you use these practices when you get out of balance?

A. First, I need to say that having out-of-balance moments is part of being human. And accepting that we all have these moments makes it a lot easier to move back in the right direction when we notice. A student at a retreat recently said, "It seems like you have such compassion." I replied, "Yes, that's true. Here, I'm being fed, housed, and supported by twenty-five people who want to be here and are enjoying the work. But, if I'm at home, tired at the end of a long day with a cranky child and demanding husband, I may not be the nicest person. I may even yell and get upset if pushed beyond the limits of that moment. The key is to recognize I have reached my limit and to stop so I may come back into balance. This might look like taking a moment to feel my feet on the floor, my backbone, or to breathe deeply and slowly all the way to the core of my bones. It works wonders to remember and choose something more life enhancing in that moment.

We all have times when we are at our best and other times when we need to rest. But life doesn't always give us the opportunity and our culture doesn't value rest. So when I am out of balance, I stop and ask, "What do I need most right now?" If I need to rest, I stop and relax. If it's my blood sugar, I'll have something to eat. Things always look better once my blood sugar has normalized. I listen to my basic sensory cues. If the atmosphere around me is too loud and my system needs quiet, I'll go for a walk. Or if I need clarity around an issue, I'll ground and fill by taking ten minutes to listen to my *Basic Relaxation and Energizing Exercise CD*. It's my favorite because by the end of that time, any foggy issue usually becomes clear.

Q. How do you balance planning with remaining open to opportunity?

A. Over the last twenty years, I have consciously chosen to live my life in a flow that stays in the present moment as much as possible. When I am in the present moment, I am open to new and unexpected opportunity when it arises. When one is worried about the future or held back by the past, it is more difficult to have the openness and flexibility that comes with living in the present. For example, I structure my work days so I see clients in the mornings, when my energy is the highest. When I finish, I am hungry and ready for lunch. But, I have plenty of energy to do what needs to be done in the afternoon—writing, marketing, and so on.

I also make it a practice to listen to my inner wisdom and make a change if something is too draining. Or I can tune in and add something that really makes my heart sing.

Q. If you received $100,000, how would you spend it?
A. I see money as a form of energy. Given this amount of energy, I would sit in meditation until I could sense where this energy would be used for the highest good.

But in this moment, here's what I think. First, I would set up a nationwide well baby care program that starts by teaching moms how to take care of themselves and how to choose their pregnancies when they are ready and able to care for an infant. This would include dads as well. This would proceed into an overhaul of the labor and delivery process, so that moms are supported in giving birth in ways that are as noninvasive, but as safe as possible.

After the moms have been assisted in connecting with their new babies (for instance, facilitating breast feeding by treating infants with poor sucking reflexes), I would finish the program with CranioSacral Therapy training for neonatal and delivery room nurses, so every baby could be treated at least once before leaving the hospital. Having well-trained CST practitioners gently remove trauma and restrictions from babies' systems would negate the need for more invasive

SUZANNE SCURLOCK-DURANA

treatments (such as giving drugs for colic) and help correct problems that could have appeared later in life. This would result in healthier, more resilient children.

Another idea is to create a national television program called *The Body Whispers* in which advanced body therapists would treat clients, showing how to listen to the body and facilitate healing. The general public has no idea that many body workers experience miracles every day as part of what they do. I have been able to help adults and children with everything from chronic illness to disability to birth injury. My clients often ask, "How do people heal who don't receive bodywork after a trauma or surgery?" This show would help more people find the healing they need in their lives.

Q. If you had thirty seconds with someone in an elevator, what three things would you tell the person to do to be joyful, peaceful, and whole?

A. Feel gratitude for what you do have in your life. Let your heart open to what is around you that is nurturing and life enhancing. These things can bring you joy if you are open to receiving. Breathe as deeply and as easily as you can. Feel your feet on the ground and the heavens about you.

Take your time. Don't let anyone rush your natural inner rhythm. Find a life's work that suits that rhythm and allows you to bring forward your inner gifts.

Q: What books or resources have helped you the most? Why?

A. I have read hundreds of helpful books in all areas of healing and living life more fully. At this moment, the ones that stand out are:

On relationships, *I like How Can I Get Through to You?* and *The New Rules of Marriage*, by Terrence Real.

On the nature of God, I like *The Shack*, by William Paul Young.

On brain physiology and conscious awareness, I like *The Mindful Brain* and *The Developing Mind*, by Daniel Siegel.

On Buddhism, I like *Pointing Out the Great Way*, by Daniel Brown.

On healing, forgiveness, and reconciliation, I like *I Thought We'd Never Speak Again*, by Laura Davis and *The Courage to Heal*, by Laura Davis and Ellen Bass.

We are blessed to be living in a time where so many authors, artists and musicians are creating works to help us wake up and feel the joy of life!

On the issue of resources in general, in my *Grounding and Healthy Boundaries* seminar, we ask students, "What is in your world right now that deeply nourishes you in a healthy way? 'Healthy' is defined as something that enhances your sense of aliveness." This question always sparks a lively discussion, and helps people recognize the healthy resources they have all around. From their responses, we have gathered a list of over five hundred resources, including activities such as walking, dancing, hiking, making love, eating good food, sitting in meditation or prayer, and creating a daily gratitude list. No two classes end up with the same list, although there is always overlap on the basics. For example, students in Miami list things like walking on the beach, while students in Canada list things like enjoying the snow, followed by a sauna. What enhances my joy is watching people's transformation, their opening and healing as a result of what I have been able to facilitate.

Q. What would you like to be written on your tombstone?
A. I've never really thought about this question. I'm only fifty-five years old and feel fairly young and foolish right now. And

SUZANNE SCURLOCK-DURANA

this may be a moot point, as I may donate my body to science. However, if I had a tombstone, I would want something about love, relationships, and connection. The way I love others and receive love in turn. You really caught me cold on this one!

Q. Anything else?

A. I'm delighted to have my book, *Full Body Presence*, written and published. I teach mainly from an oral tradition, researching a topic, creating a rough outline and then letting Spirit pour through with whatever I need to say. So writing at this length and detail, then editing and re-editing, was quite a discipline. However, I'm now much more comfortable with letting my gifts come through my writing. A door has opened for me and I find myself doing lots of it. So I have deep gratitude for this writing initiation that *Full Body Presence* has allowed me to experience.

One more thought. I highly encourage people to integrate any healing bodywork they may be receiving with the principles of healthy body presence. Receiving good bodywork makes it easier to have this presence. And when you know these principles—how energy moves through the body and how it operates optimally—you are able to incorporate the bodywork you receive more easily, deeply, and lastingly. Retaining the gains you make in your healing sessions is almost effortless when you practice the skills of full body presence. Enjoy!

"I make this sound to give the whole world peace."
**Shree Krishna Shahi, Tibetan Singing Bowl Therapist
and Sound Healer**

Shree Krishna Shahi was the first person in the Kathmandu valley of Nepal to work with Tibetan singing bowls. He learned about the bowls from his adopted Tibetan grandfather, Tashi Lama, who came to Nepal during the winters in the early 1980s. Through his sound studies with the elder monk, Shree learned the traditional secrets of singing bowl therapy and sound healing. He started to understand the interconnections among the chakras, planets, metals, colors, and tones and how working with the Tibetan singing bowls could enhance people's health and well-being.

For twenty years, Shree has been using the Tibetan singing bowls to give sound therapy, teach students, and perform concerts. He has toured worldwide, and with Santa Ratna Shakya, has formed Tibetan Singing Bowl centers in Germany, America, Nepal, and other Asian countries. Peter Hess and Hans de Back, now famous in their own right, are both Shree's students. Shree works and teaches at the Old Tibet store http://www.oldtibet.com/ in Boulder, Colorado during the summer. He lives in the Swayambhunath Stupa in Kathmandu, Nepal.

Q. What experiences put you on your spiritual path?

A. When I was a boy, a Tibetan salt trader and lama named Tashi used to come to my town in Nepal for the winter. One day, I returned home from school and saw my mom buying salt from him. He had many bowls of different sizes, which he used to measure the salt. I accidentally kicked the bowls over while looking for something to eat. They made an incredible sound. Tashi was angry and my mother said, "Why

SHREE KRISHNA SHAHI

did you do that? Say you are sorry." I was too scared to look at him so I said sorry to my mother. After making the sound, I forgot about my hunger and just wanted to hear it one more time. When Tashi turned his back, I kicked the bowls again. This time, my mother and he were both livid. They checked the bowls to make sure they weren't broken. Then, I apologized to him, shaking with fear because I thought he might hurt me.

For almost a week, I avoided going near his teepee, even though I loved to hear the sound of his horse bell. Then, while walking home one afternoon, he smiled and offered me some tsampa, flat bread with salt and butter. I was scared and tried to take it without getting too close but he caught my hand and pulled me into his lap. I screamed to my mother but quickly calmed down as he was kind to me and the tsampa tasted good. From that day on, I began smiling at him.

I asked my mother if she could buy me one of his bowls. She asked Tashi and he said, "Your son is like my grandchild. I will give him one of the bowls." He also gave me a small stick to strike it with. I was the only one in Nepal who had a Tibetan singing bowl and I was grateful to Tashi for giving it to me. I came to regard him as my adopted Tibetan grandfather. I looked forward to his return every winter so I could spend time with him and learn more about the bowls.

When I turned fifteen, Tashi taught me how to make a meditation sound with the bowls. The first time I tried, I made many mistakes but, a year later, I could play one bowl well. At age seventeen, I played the bowl and tears of joy began streaming down my face. Tashi said, "It's time to teach you how to play four bowls and a tingshaw [high-pitched cymbals] for total body balancing." I lay down and he placed one bowl above my head, two at my sides, and one between my legs. Then, as he played the bowls and tingshaw, I relaxed into a deep sleep. When I awoke, Tashi said, "Don't give these bowls to anyone. They are for you to help people and yourself." So, I started giving sessions to my neighbors, friends, and others in the valley.

By age nineteen, tourists who had heard about my work with the Tibetan singing bowls started approaching me for free lessons and healing. A year later, Tashi showed me how to use the bowls for both chakra and warm water therapy. After these teachings, he said, "You are now well trained and can help the whole world." By age twenty-two, I became known throughout Nepal as the "King of the Singing Bowl." People began coming from all over the globe to see me.

Tashi realized I needed to reach more people so the last time he came, he brought me three more bowls. With these, I had seven, plus the tingshaw, to do sound therapy and give peace concerts. People were so relaxed after these concerts. The sound helped clear their minds and emotional blocks, and connected their hearts and souls. In general, balancing therapy helps with pain, stress, tension, headaches, insomnia, depression, and fatigue.

The next winter, Tashi did not come. I went over to the others who had made the trip and asked where he was. They told me that my adopted grandfather had passed away. They then gave me his last bowl, which they had carried all the way from Tibet. I shed many tears as I prayed and lit candles to thank him for all he had given me. I told him I was sorry I was not there at the end of his days.

Q. How did these experiences change you?
A. After Tashi's passing, my life began again as a singing bowl therapist and sound healer. I never expected to play the singing bowls because, before I met my adopted grandfather, I loved the guitar and wanted to pursue that. But at age forty-six, I'm still working with the bowls, giving free therapy and

SHREE KRISHNA SHAHI

213

concerts around the world. It's my life's work and I will do it until I die. My focus now is passing this knowledge onto others so they can share it with as many people as possible. The singing bowl gives life forever.

Q. What changes are others noticing about you?

A. Many of my students say, "Shree, you look the same as when I met you twenty years ago." I tell them it is because sound therapy keeps me young like an evergreen tree. It gives me energy so I never feel old.

Q. What changes are you noticing about your life and the world?

A. Even though the sound keeps me young, I am getting older. That's why I feel an even greater need to pass this knowledge onto others. In Europe, many of my former students now work as sound therapists. Some have even published books on the subject. This is what I have waited my whole life to see. When I die, I know the sound will be there for future generations. It's important because it really works. By playing just four notes on the bowls and striking the tingshaw, I can help someone with insomnia to fall asleep, or someone with memory loss to remember. Often, tears of joy stream down people's faces as the sound cleanses their bodies and helps them feel light, peaceful, and happy.

Q. What has been the most challenging part of your path?

A. When I was eight years old, my father died. I started working to help support the family. I worked everywhere from vegetable and fruit shops to restaurants and cowboy ranches. This was a hard time in my life and my mother's, too, because she had to care for all we children. My mother was happy when I later became a healer. I was happy too because I could help her and so many others. I will continue to do sound therapy for the rest of my life because helping people makes my family and me happy. So there have been challenges, but they were worth it because I am here now.

Q. What is your earliest memory? Why do you remember it?

A. When I was six years old, my older brother used to tease
me by saying, "You have eyes like a 'queery.'" "Queery" is a
Nepalese slang term for European man. Whenever he called
me this, I secretly liked it. I did look European because I was
fair-skinned. I also remember injuring my head several times
during accidents. I recall feeling how much my mother loved
me as she treated my wounds with herbal remedies. In general, I have so many good memories of my mother, siblings,
and adopted grandfather.

Q. Who are your mentors? What have you learned from them?

A. My mentor was my adopted Tibetan grandfather, Tashi, who
was a lama, shaman, and singing bowl and drum healer. He
was a wonderful man who taught me everything I know
about sound therapy. He lived a simple life, riding into Nepal
every winter on his horse and staying in his teepee, which
was large enough for thirty people. To stay warm, he lit a fire
inside and slept under yak skin. He never took much money
for his salt, preferring to trade for items such as wheat, rice,
and corn. At age seventy, he cut a striking figure—tall, hand-
some, and healthy like an American Indian. He even had all
his teeth because he ate only natural food out of the singing
bowls. In Tibetan and Nepali culture, people often eat and
drink out of these bowls because they contain seven essential metals that have healing properties: copper, iron, lead,
tin, mercury, silver, and gold. The G bowl, corresponding to
the third chakra, is especially good for the stomach.

Q. What is the greatest challenge facing society?

A. People work too hard. This creates tension and stress as they
get stuck in their heads and feel unsatisfied. I want to share
this sound with the world to help people relax and feel peace.
I often work with persons who are living with HIV/AIDS. They
sometimes have darkness in their minds because they worry
so much about their lives. I give them sound therapy by put-

SHREE KRISHNA SHAHI

ting the singing bowls on their bodies to create pain reliev-ing vibrations. After ten minutes, they forget they have the disease. This is because the therapy clears their minds, calms their nervous systems, and eases their discomfort. One of my students with HIV/AIDS now works as a sound therapist helping others with the disease. Doing the work gives him greater mental peace and purpose so he can continue on with his life. I also instruct classes and give peace concerts all over the world, especially in Europe. Some of our concerts have been recorded on CD.

In addition, I have had the honor to share this sound with world leaders. For example, I gave a concert at the Dalai Lama's monastery. He is a remarkable person whose pres-ence brings peace and kindness. When the Clinton's visited the Swayambhunath Stupa where I live in Nepal, I played the bowls for their daughter Chelsea. She liked the sound so much, she returned twice to hear them. She bought a bowl and I also gave her a bell. When the Democratic conven-tion was in Denver last summer, Barak Obama's close friend stopped by the Old Tibet store where I work looking for a headache remedy. I told him we did not have one but I could do singing bowl therapy with him. He lay down and, after only a few minutes, fell asleep. When he awoke, his head-ache was gone and he felt very relaxed. Shortly thereafter, he brought his whole family in for therapy.

Q. What advice would you give someone just starting his or her spiritual path?

A. Don't worry about anything you have a problem with in your life. Jesus is always behind you, supporting you. When you need food, he will give you some. You will not go hungry. When I see beggars at the temple or homeless people on the street, I always want to help by passing on what I have. Even if I have only a little bread, just enough for me, I share it. Once I give the bread, I feel happy and satisfied because I have supported someone.

TIBETAN SINGING BOWL THERAPIST

This is my great interest—to support as many people as I can. Each morning, when I walk out the door, I pray to God saying, "Please forgive me if I cause harm or pain." I also pray to not be angry, deceitful, or hurtful. I just want to help by smiling, talking to people, and giving sound therapy. This is my dream and it is coming true. Now, I pray for the whole world to experience peace. We need to work together to make this happen. That's how we will live in this world.

Q. Anything else?

A. I love to play the singing bowls for senior citizens and children with disabilities. When I played at a school for the handicapped in India, the students were so happy. I receive the same response from deaf children who can feel the bowls' vibrations. Recently, I gave a peace concert at a nursing home in Colorado. Many of the seniors there have difficulties with their minds. But when they heard the sound, they started to smile, some for the first time in years. They probably also had less trouble sleeping that night. Helping people in this way makes me so happy.

Q. What do you think of the concept that my enemy is my lover?

A. I like it because on one side, you have the enemy and, on the other, you have the lover. They are equal. It is a nice way to think about it.

SHREE KRISHNA SHAHI

217

"I Choose Love."

- Shawn Gallaway

"There is the known, the unknown, and the unknowable."

Mukunda Stiles, Author and Director of the Yoga Therapy Center

Mukunda Stiles is the author of *Structural Yoga Therapy*, *Yoga Sutras of Patanjali*, *Ayurvedic Yoga Therapy*, and *Tantrik Yoga Secrets*. He is a spiritual mentor and gives trainings in Boulder, Colorado, Amsterdam, the Netherlands, and Ganeshpuri, India. For more information, please visit the Yoga Therapy Center at: www.yogatherapycenter.org.

Q. What experiences put you on your spiritual path?

A. I had a profound experience the very first time I did yoga. I was drafted during Vietnam and put into the army's prep school for West Point Military Academy. While in school, a friend found a yoga book and I said with curiosity, "Let's do what it says." The book stated that yogis could control their minds and slow down and even stop their respiration and heart. I tried to do this and was successful without a mentor—something I would not encourage today. I went out of my body for an hour, hovering at the ceiling while looking down at my physical form lying on the floor. This gave me the lasting realization that I am not my body. For the next few years, I experienced several paranormal phenomena: past life readings, spontaneously healing others, astral travel, and being in the state called *Samadhi* while in the company of an omnipresent spirit. Looking back, I would say I started out on the path of the Yoga Sutras, which is about psychic abilities that arise from spiritual awakening. The Yoga Sutras are the guidebook for yoga as a spiritual practice.

Four years later, I met my spiritual teacher, Baba Muktananda, who helped me understand the spontaneous experiences I'd had and gave me a spiritual practice to stabilize and deepen my connection to Spirit. The practices of Tantrik Yoga that my guru gave helped me live an integrated spiritual and worldly lifestyle. Being with him and our spiritual group gave community to my life as my guru began to unite with an inner teacher that formerly was my intuition. I have always felt in their presence and am guided moment to moment. Sri Aurobindo said, "Yoga is condensed evolution." I felt the truth of those words every day and continue to do so. Muktananda confirmed that I was a yogi, saying, "Make that your livelihood." He gave me his blessings to mentor others and give spiritual initiations.

Q. How did these experiences change you?

A. The first several years involved a heightening of psychic intuition and discrimination about who to be with and how to guide others. I did not experience a physical change until my guru told me to seek training with B. K. S. Iyengar. From 1975 to 1976, I went through an Iyengar teacher training course and lived with my instructor, Rama Jyoti Vernon. After the course I did advanced study in anatomy and kinesiology, which led to creating a structural change to my knocked knees. My *Structural Yoga Therapy* book came out of this process, showing how to assess weakened muscles that cause pain and structural distortion such as scoliosis. I created the method in the late 1970s, but didn't write the book until 2000. My guru used to say, "You need to know three levels beyond what you are teaching." So I waited twenty years to mature enough to explain the levels of healing beyond the physical—meditation and spiritual training.

Q. What changes are you noticing about your life and the world?

A. In my early life, I never really fit in. Even though I hung out with the guys on my long-distance running team, I always felt like an outsider. When I graduated from college, I didn't know what to do. When my guru told me to become a full-time yoga teacher, I thought, *Yeah*. I really felt the validity

Yoga Therapy Center (side margin)

of doing that with my life. Before that, I didn't think it was possible because there were very few full-time yogis in the 1970s, the exceptions being my teachers Rama Jyoti Vernon, B.K.S. Iyengar, and Indra Devi.

My vision of myself as a yoga teacher is much broader than what is offered in teacher trainings today. Yoga has become a fitness and paramedical industry. It's not Classical Yoga, the tradition that incorporates working with our multidimensional body, mind, and spirit the way my spiritual teachers instructed. Now I have written four books and have two more in process. They started with the *Yoga Sutras*, which I consider the guidebook for all on a spiritual path. The other books progress from the gross self to deeper dimensions of mind and spirit, as based on the *Sutras*, which were written before Christ. To me, being a yogi means to follow that book and my spiritual teacher. When my guru died in 1982, I had to rely much more on the book. So I worked on a poetic rendition of it for nearly twenty years until my inner teacher was satisfied. I discovered that the presence of God/Goddess is knowing the true self as omnipresent consciousness and feeling the commonality of all spiritual paths. This feeling of devotion is central to all spiritual paths, especially Classical Yoga.

That larger perspective guides and directs me even if the client comes to see me for *structural yoga therapy* when faced with chronic physical pain that nothing else has helped. The tendency is to forget the bigger picture. Yoga texts state pain and suffering are real and the actions, thoughts, and feelings that we have move us to deal with that reality. Removing pain is part one. Part two is understanding that your lifestyle causes this pain. Part three is submission to receiving help to be free of the causes of pain and suffering. It is moving past the known to the unknown and persisting at knowing even the unknowable. The known is our comfort zone, the unknown is why there is pain and suffering, and the unknowable is the true self as Spirit. The deeper teachings of yoga are to understand who we are.

Through self-awareness, illness and injury just fall away and their relative significance in the bigger picture is realized. In the beginning of my thirty-five years as a yoga teacher, I took a purely physical approach with people. Structural yoga therapy focused on addressing their poor posture and muscular weakness with a personalized program that made even chronic pain diminish. Now I realize that the problem is a conditioning of mind that lacks serenity and seeks it instead in outward activity. So today I train teachers and therapists to be competent with that so they can go beyond physical considerations to help promote a healthy lifestyle and spiritual practice. When clients perceive themselves as spiritual seekers, they put attention on their inner life. They find that meditation—and the resulting transformation of self-perception—promotes serenity no matter what life throws at them. Instead of looking for stress, the mind looks for serenity and presence. We always find what we diligently seek.

Q. What changes are others noticing about you?

A. The comment I often get from my family is that I am at peace. I wasn't so much early in life. They also say my features and body look the same as when I was a teenager—same height, weight, physique, and playful manner. But I have been doing yoga now for forty years, so it is hard to say much other than this is my yoga life. Since age twenty, I have never really had a life outside of yoga. I currently live part-time in three countries: India, Holland, and the U.S. Even with a busy schedule of teaching and writing, I am content. Adjusting to life is relatively easy when Spirit is present.

Q. What has been the most challenging part of your path?

A. Relationships. I have had lots of challenges in that arena. So I struggle with being stable in them. It has taken me my whole

YOGA THERAPY CENTER

life to accept that my relationships are short-lived. Not just intimate ones, but also those with spiritual teachers. I spent eight years with each of my teachers, so these were the longest lasting. But even those were there for a while and then went away. Relating to Spirit is easier for me. Tantra Yoga, Kundalini Yoga, and the esoteric literature and treatises are all easy for me. However, my relationship challenges have given me a tremendous capacity to persevere and love myself—so much so that I am feeling optimistic about the love relationship I'm in now. The challenges and spiritual practices have guided me into a more fulfilling relationship that has taken the form of a Tantrik consort. We are in a committed partnership whose purpose is to help each other with relationship to Spirit—to see the divine in each other and to love that one.

Q. What is your earliest memory? Why do you remember it?

A. Before I trained in rebirthing, I had little memory of my early childhood other than flashes of recollection from pictures my mother had. Once I trained in continuous Tantrik energy practice—which is a continuous *pranayama* or breathing with no pauses—early traumatic childhood memories and past life memories began to surface. I was in two earthquakes as a child, one when I was a few months old and the other when I was two years old. My parents didn't respond well to those earthquakes. In the first one, my mother ran out of the building, leaving me alone inside. That certainly colored my early life and led to my fear of abandonment in intimate relationships. In the second, my sister's crib got knocked over in the middle of the night and my father ran into her room, accidentally kicking me in the stomach as I lay on the floor. So I got a tremendous contraction in my solar plexus and diaphragm as a result. Through yoga and rebirthing, that frozen breath, that stuck moment in time, was released.

The main process of yoga is to be free of all stress and ten-

MUKUNDA STILES

sion no matter where it originated, even from past lives. I am now at peace with these traumas and feel that relations with my parents have never been better.

Q. Who are your mentors? What have you learned from them?
A. I have had two groups: my spiritual teachers and my physical yoga teachers. They taught very different systems of Classical Yoga. Muktananda, my spiritual guru, did not give us physical practices—Hatha Yoga poses—until the end of his life. For the first seven years, we did no *asanas* and no *pranayama*. Before I met him, I had done some *asanas* with an American named Paul Copeland, who had studied with a great master, Professor T. Krishnamacharya, in India. Paul, an aspiring physician, was given a set of practices that I have written up in the *Ayurvedic Yoga Therapy* book that were flowing posture sequences, or *vinyasas*, with *prana* enlivening practices for expanded intelligence.

I also had a spiritual teacher in the Muktananda lineage named Swami Prakashananda. He was a Tantrik teacher like my guru, but he was more of a devotional Tantrik—being devoted to Divine Mother. Through him, I learned the humility approach to Tantra whereas, through Muktananda, I learned the Kundalini approach, which also incorporated text study. In Kundalini, ecstatic experiences were common occurrences that resulted from spontaneous energy awakening (*shaktipat*), emotional release of suppressed feelings, and captivating visions. The purification aspect of yoga is well documented and this process I went thorough extended it to the multi dimensions of body, psyche, and spirit. In contrast to Muktananda's, the Tantra practices were sweet, gentle, and comforting. I have been with many Indian teachers, most notably Ammachi, the hugging woman guru, who I highly recommend. But none of them has led me to the depths that these two teachers did.

In the Hatha Yoga world, Rama Jyoti has been the most influential. She has been my teacher for thirty-five years and we still phone each other fairly often. She was a student of B. K. S. Iyengar as well as Kundalini teachers. Indra Devi, another disciple of Krishnamacharya, has also been my teacher. She studied with him in 1938 and died in 2002 three weeks shy of her 103rd birthday. I went to her hundredth birthday party in Buenos Aires. She was pretty much a devotional teacher, yet in the physical, or Hatha Yoga, tradition.

Q. What is the greatest challenge facing society?

A. It's lack of faith in God, a lack of devotion. Spiritual presence is always with us. Calamities such as the economy and war don't mean that God/Goddess isn't here. For people who aren't devotional, they can be Jnânas. Jnâna Yoga is the path of wisdom. It helps us understand what consciousness, the mind, and life are all about. In that regard, my guru's teachings have been a great boon, as he encouraged study of the wisdom texts, especially *The Yoga Vasistha*. This book literally talks the reader into an illuminated state of consciousness. That need to search for Spirit is something everybody is doing every moment. But we require the help of a spiritual teacher who can point out that our search for satisfaction is really a search for that part of ourselves that is naturally satisfied to begin with. You can't get satisfaction if it is external because that means it can go away. If you can attain it, you can lose it. It's through the Jnâna Yoga path that we transform our perception of the world. That transformation makes the world a beautiful place filled with grace, delight, and astonishment.

Q. What advice would you give someone just starting his or her spiritual path?

A. Everyone is on a spiritual path. Spirit is the inner voice that constantly calls to us. When we listen, it keeps our inner teacher close and brings us to an outer teacher who can help us realize the omnipresent teacher. That relationship encourages us to be fulfilled in all areas of life. The great

MUKUNDA STILES

sage Ramana Maharshi said, "I give people what they want so they will be open to receiving what I have to give." This is a nice strategy.

In the beginning years, a lot of people wanted my help to lessen physical pain. Now, I don't get as many of those clients. But when I do, I still start with their pain. Currently, the majority of people who come to my workshops or read my books see that I have deeper teachings to offer. They come seeking help for how to live a spiritual life integrated with daily existence, and for help with relationships. Isn't that a surprise? The one who has challenges in relationship gets to give advice about what he has learned. To a great degree, all relationships are about knowing ourselves.

So, the advice I give is this. First, I want people to see that life is about making the right efforts (*tapasya*) so that their conditioned mind will always seek Spirit and their inner teacher. I want them to understand that the struggle they are engaged in, whatever it is, is to purify them. The word *"tapas"* means to heat up, to purify, to burn away karma. Second, I tell people to find a tradition that attracts them and to study its texts, whether they be in the Bible, the Yoga Sutras, the Torah, or the Koran. If it really speaks to them, then it's a way to higher consciousness. Third, I believe it's important to commit oneself to working directly with a teacher, a mentor who can bring the texts to life and help people see that their difficulties, as well as their blessings, are their spiritual path. We can receive grace from a deceased teacher but only a living one can embody the spiritual life.

Those three elements are from the Yoga Sutras and my favorite book, *The Yoga Vasistha*. The Vasistha is similar to the Buddha's story and to Arjuna's in the Bhagavad Gita. It's a fabulous text that helps people recognize and resolve life's fundamental paradox: its apparent chaos and pointlessness (maya) and its divine significance. Through reflecting on the

Yoga Therapy Center

text, our minds become conditioned to persistently seek and manifest self-realization.

Q. What are your practices for connecting to your higher purpose?

A. I have done many different spiritual practices, or *sadhanas*, over the years. Each practice produces a specific result delineated in the yoga texts. Once the attainment arises, it is best to do a new *sadhana* guided by a mentor. I did four to six hours of physical yoga a day until I wrote the *Structural Yoga Therapy* book. Once I understood the purpose of that *sadhana*, I didn't need to do as much Hatha Yoga. When writing other teachings, such as the *Ayurvedic Yoga Therapy* book, I did *vinyasa* from Krishnamacharya for an hour a day and the *pranayamas* associated with it for another half hour. In the ashram, we did three hours of chanting, an hour of scripture reading, and an hour of mediation each day. Also, my guru's teachings were to chant a mantra and meditate, as well as do accessory mantras for purifying the mind.

Now, I spend much more time with the meditation and study of the Vasistha and Yoga Sutras and some other important supplemental texts. These texts are about turning around my mind. It's a continuous practice. If I am not reading a text, then I am reflecting on it. If I'm not doing an asana, then I'm watching people to see how I can help them be more comfortable in their bodies.

Q. How do you use these practices when you get out of balance?

A. My mother is struggling with age, my brother is struggling with finances, and my teacher is struggling with home foreclosures. All these things cause worry and anxiety. The illusion of life, maya, is not something I can just dismiss. Life is also a divine play with lessons to be learned. So I meditate, read the Vasistha's Yoga, give money, and help out where appropriate.

MUKUNDA STILES

I also work with the foundational evolutionary qualities of Ayurveda, called the *doshas*. Vata practice leads to serenity, pitta practice to discrimination, and kapha practice to love. So if I am not feeling peaceful, I do more vata practice. If I am not making good decisions, I do more pitta practice. If I am not being compassionate, I do more kapha practice. That's the simple trinity of balancing the *doshas*. These practices are in my new book *Ayurveda Yoga Therapy*. How we do them varies according to how we react to the world on a particular day.

When life is especially painful, I quit work and go on a pilgrimage, or *yatra*, with no goal. In general, my practice is to seek Spirit's guidance and let it direct me. This technique evolved over time. First I would surrender to the moment. Then I would surrender for minutes, hours, days, and then months. I have made a habit of this pilgrimage practice and it has moved my life in grace-filled ways that I never could have anticipated. For example, I have taken a break from teaching four times, ranging from four to ten months, to let Spirit lead me. This practice is the deepest one I have ever experienced.

Q. How do you balance planning with remaining open to opportunity?

A. Right now, it is about persistently listening to my inner teacher, my consciousness, and my consort's advice. I'm trying to be in a creative mode to finish my latest book. When I am in this mode, my schedule is flexible so I can stay in a contemplative mind frame. I am a person who maintains discipline, but not consistently. I'll do it for three months and then take a few weeks off to evolve into my next *sadhana* (which involves taking a different approach). I believe in moderation in all areas of life.

Yoga Therapy Center

Q. If you received $100,000, how would you spend it?

A. Money comes and goes easily in my life. I've had a good amount and I don't have as much now. This is because I'm sixty and choose to live simply without working as much as I did in recent periods. My partner and I live in a small condo in Amsterdam. Just before this, I lived in an enormous house in western Massachusetts. In six months, I have gone to the opposite end of the pole. So it's more about being content with what life brings. For example, when I teach in New York, I often walk down the street with a pocket full of twenty-dollar bills thinking, *Who does this belong to?* when it doesn't feel like it belongs to me.

I support three charitable funds in India that would certainly get a chunk of the money. They are all near my guru's, and my spiritual teacher's, ashrams. In Ganeshpuri, where my guru Muktananda lived, there is a program that teaches local people organic gardening, and another that gives children better access to computers, English language skills, and happiness. Likewise, my spiritual teacher, Prakashananda, founded an ashram for young boys, which also provides education and lunch to all the children in the village. I plan to go to India regularly in the winter to give teachings, as well as my time and income.

Q. If you had thirty seconds with someone in an elevator, what three things would you tell him or her to do to be joyful, peaceful, and whole?

A. If I had only thirty seconds, I'd first make eye contact, smile, and say, "God/Goddess is with you no matter what." Second, I'd build rapport and generate a reflective mood in them by saying, "The world is as you see it. If you are not seeing it clearly, it will be stressful. So, if you can see the world from an elevated point of view—and perhaps I can provide that for you in this moment—then you can see your situation more clearly." Third, I would repeat what I first said and wish them well.

MUKUNDA STILES

Q. What books or resources have helped you the most? Why?

A. As far as books, for those with a rapport to my yogic path, I would suggest a couple of books by my guru, Muktananda: *Meditate: Happiness Lies Within You* and *Where Are You Going?: A Guide to the Spiritual Journey*. For someone who has been searching but is not satisfied with the search, then I would suggest another book he wrote called *Play of Consciousness: A Spiritual Autobiography*. For those really committed to spiritual practice, the main one is *Vasistha's Yoga* by the translator Swami Venkatesananda. In addition, anything by or about Ramana Maharshi is phenomenal. A good starting one is *The Spiritual Teachings of Ramana Maharshi*, which has a preface by Carl Jung. There is a much more extensive recommended reading list on my website from all traditions.

Q. What would you like to be written on your tombstone?

A. I don't wish to have a tombstone. My mother has a plot for me and says I can use it. I might. I don't know. I'm close to my parents. They are very sweet, good people. As time goes on, India becomes more and more my spiritual home. So I'd probably have my ashes tossed into the river there.

The books I am writing will have a life of their own after I'm gone, but it won't be for long. There are always new books and insights coming out. So I'm hopeful that while I'm around, these books will help people. I love receiving beautiful greeting cards from readers who tell me how the teachings of Classical Yoga and spiritual life have made a difference in their lives. I save these treasures for periodic upliftment.

Q. Anything else?

A. It's important to search for a spiritual mentor who can help you see that you are on a unique path. Even if you don't find one, that search will help you remain close to your inner teacher. I like to distinguish between a spiritual guru and spiritual teachers and institutions. A spiritual teacher gives you lessons that they received from their teacher. If you need a more defined path, then you should look at institutions of yoga and spiritual life that can provide that. However, a spiritual guru is someone who unexpectedly shows up as a result of your searching the other two categories.

One of my best teachers is a crazy hippy living in the redwood forests of Northern California named Yogi Hal. He saw the world this way: there's the known, the unknown, and the unknowable. The known mentor helps you understand what you have a pretty good grasp of but don't quite get. The unknown is a spiritual teacher who shows you knowledge and wisdom about what you don't know that is known by someone else. The guru is someone who helps you find the unknowable. Really look for the unknowable, because it is through this humility that spiritual life stays alive. Through the other types of teachings, it becomes dead. We kill Spirit as soon as we think we know it. Spiritual life is meant to be a wonder, a mystery, and some confusion. We're already doing this. We just need help from one who can bring these teachings into the situations that make up our life.

MUKUNDA STILES

ACKNOWLEDGEMENTS

I would like to thank the following people who have made a difference in my life. To Celina Moore Barton, Stephany Buchicchio, Jennifer Stark, Geetanjali Chander, Signe Kurian, and Ruby Mayeda for being true friends and for teaching me about love. To Nancy Mercer, Barry Kopecky, Peter Rutland, Tony Daley, Robert J. Thomas, and Denise Darringrand for being outstanding teachers and mentors. To Dr. John Upledger, Dr. Charles Radbill, Dr. Jim Kerner, Jamy Faust, and Felice Lazarus for being exceptional healers and for helping me recover from my injury. To Rev. Diana Peters at Intercession Episcopal Church and Donna Visocky and Linda Potter at BellaSpark Productions for being spiritual lights and for giving me the chance to write. To Gary Zukav, Linda Francis, and everyone in the Authentic Power Program for being in spiritual partnership with me and for helping me live courageously. To my CranioSacral Therapy clients for teaching me so much about beingness. To my grandmother Sophia, my husband Jasper, and my son Trevor for being so supportive and loving.

I also would like to thank all the spiritual leaders who generously gave their time to participate in this project. Their wisdom, courage, and willingness to share made this book possible. I especially am grateful to Brian Schwartz, Founder of 50 Interviews, for giving me the opportunity to author this book, Penney Peirce, renowned intuitive and author, for writing such an incisive forward, and Melanie Mulhall, shaman and editor, for doing a marvelous editing job, and Dave Block, Cofounder of Make-it-Fly, for introducing me to Brian.

Finally, I would like to express my heartfelt gratitude to spiritual leaders, past and present, who inspire me every day: Jesus, Buddha, Lao Tzu, the Dalai Lama, Mother Teresa, Gandhi, Saint Teresa of Ãvila, Saint John of the Cross, The Desert Fathers, Mungo Park, Joan of Arc, Stanford Addison, Christopher Reeve, Dick and Rick Hoyt, and the people of Nepal, Tibet, and China.

I send love and gratitude to all sentient beings. We are one. Thank you, Tuula Fai

ABOUT THE AUTHOR

Tuula Hoiska Fai is an author, speaker, seminar leader, and CranioSacral Therapist with fifteen years of experience in the human development field. She is the author of the highly acclaimed book, *Seek the Lover Within*. This book is the first in the 50 Interview series. Tuula gives presentations around the world on spirituality, personal growth, and healing to audiences including corporations, civic organizations, and individuals. Her passion is helping people achieve a state of oneness in which they follow their calling and devote their lives to service. Her own journey began when a debilitating all-over body injury encouraged her to heal herself holistically almost twenty years ago. You can contact her at tuula@tuulafai.com.

Prior to this work, Tuula was a marketing director and management consultant for Fortune 500 companies such as IBM, Oracle, and KPMG. She earned her MBA from Georgetown and her BA from Wesleyan University.

Stay up to date with Tuula and her latest interviews through her blog

spiritual.50interviews.com

Tuula Fai, MBA, CST, NCTMB
CranioSacral Therapist
303-909-4582
www.tuulafai.com
tuula@50interviews.com

ABOUT 50 INTERVIEWS

Imagine a university where not only does each student get a textbook custom tailored to a curriculum they personally designed, but where each student literally becomes the author!

The mission of 50 Interviews, Inc. is to provide aspiring, passionate, driven people a framework to achieve their dreams of becoming that which they aspire to be. Learning what it takes to be the best in your field, directly from those who have already succeeded. The ideal author is someone who desires to be a recognized expert in their field. You will be part of a community of authors who share your passion and who have learned firsthand how the 50 Interviews concept works. A form of extreme education, the process will transform you into that which you aspire to become.

50 Interviews is a publisher of books, CDs, videos, and software that serve to inform, educate, and inspire others on a wide range of topics. Timely insight, inspiration, collective wisdom, and best practices derived directly from those who have already succeeded. Authors surround themselves with those they admire, gain clarity of purpose, adopt critical beliefs, and build a network of peers to ensure success in that endeavor. Readers gain knowledge and perspective from those who have already achieved a result they desire.

If you are interested in learning more, I would love to hear from you! You can contact me via email at: brian@50interviews.com, by phone: 970-215-1078 (Colorado), or through our website:

www.50interviews.com

All my best,
Brian Schwartz
Authorpreneur and creator of *50 Interviews*

OTHER 50 INTERVIEWS TITLES

Additional topics based on the 50 Interviews model that have already been released or are in development:

Athletes over 50
By Don McGrath, Ph.D.

Successful Jobseekers
By Gordon Nuttall

Young Entrepreneurs
By Nick Tart and Nick Scheidies

Artists
By Maryann Swartz

Video Marketing Pioneers
By Randy Berry

Attraction Marketers
By Rob Christensen

Physicians in Transition
By Richard Fernandez, MD

Actors
By Stella Hannah

Scientists
By David Giltner, Ph.D.

Wealth Managers
By Allen Duck

Millionaire Women
by Kirsten McCay-Smith

Entrepreneurs
by Brian Schwartz

Property Managers
by Michael Levy

Professional Speakers
by Laura Lee Carter & Brian Schwartz

Learn more at
www.50interviews.com

LaVergne, TN USA
09 June 2010
185514LV00003B/6/P